THE B-SCHOOL SAGA

JOURNEY OF BUSINESS EDUCATION IN INDIA (1947-2025)

ASHISH GUPTA

To the dreamers, doers, and difference-makers—

To the **visionaries** who imagined institutions before they were built,
To the **educators** who chose to shape minds over balance sheets,
To the **students** from metros and mofussils who dared to dream big,
To the **entrepreneurs and leaders** who carried India forward,
And to the countless unsung **heroes in classrooms, libraries, and hostels**—
who quietly built the backbone of India's business education revolution.

This book is for you.
May your stories continue to inspire a generation.
May your legacy live on in every B-school corridor, across Bharat and beyond.

Contents

Contents

Preface

The Idea Behind This Book: The journey of business education in India is not just the story of classrooms, case studies, and corporate placements—it's a mirror to the country's economic, cultural, and intellectual evolution. As India transitioned from a colonial economy to a mixed economy, and now to a global powerhouse, business schools have played a critical yet underexplored role in shaping the minds that drive this transformation.

This book was born out of a simple observation: while India boasts of some of the world's most prestigious business institutions like the IIMs and ISB, there is little consolidated literature that traces the story of how these institutions came to be, what shaped their philosophies, who the pioneers were, and how business education has evolved in response to India's changing socio-economic context.

Over the last few decades, the Indian B-school landscape has witnessed immense growth—both in numbers and in diversity of approach. From public institutions that laid the foundation of formal management education to the rise of private players offering globalized curricula, the sector has seen innovation, expansion, and occasional turbulence. Through this book, I aim to chart this journey—not just through the lens of institutions and rankings, but through ideas, individuals, and impact.

This is not merely a historical account. It is also a reflection on how Indian business education must evolve to meet the demands of the 21st century. In an era of rapid technological disruption, climate challenges, and shifting economic paradigms, our business schools must rise beyond placement numbers and embrace their responsibility of nation-building.

"The B-School Saga" is, therefore, a tribute—to the visionaries who laid the foundation, the educators who shaped generations, the students who became changemakers, and the institutions that continue to reimagine the future of India through business education.

Let this book serve as a guide, a record, and a call to action—for educators, students, policymakers, and anyone who believes in the transformative power of education.

Ashish Gupta
Author
May 2025

Prologue

When a Nation Grows, Its Classrooms Must Lead: Every great nation has its institutions. Not just monuments of stone and steel, but places where minds are forged, leaders are built, and ideas take flight.

In India, as we transitioned from freedom to development, from struggle to strategy, and from identity to innovation, a quiet yet powerful revolution was taking shape—inside classrooms labeled MBA.

The story of Indian business education is more than a tale of rankings, campuses, and corporate salaries. It is a story of:

Aspiration – of students from every corner of India seeking transformation through education.

Vision – of policymakers and thinkers who believed that good governance and good management must go hand in hand.

Resilience – of institutions that evolved from chalkboards to smartboards, from public sector planners to global boardroom strategists.

And above all, a story of India finding its voice in the language of leadership.

From the earliest commerce colleges to the founding of the IIMs, from the liberalization-fueled private B-school boom to the rise of EdTech and hybrid MBAs, this saga captures how management education mirrored India's own economic and social evolution.

And now, as India stands on the brink of becoming a Viksit Bharat by 2047, the question before us is not just how we teach management—but how we lead through it.

This book is a chronicle of that journey.
A journey still in motion.

A saga still being written.

Welcome to The B-School Saga.

Disclaimer

This book, The B-School Saga: Journey of Business Education in India, is a work of non-fiction based on the author's professional experience, academic observations, and extensive research. It draws upon publicly available data, institutional reports, policy documents, media coverage, academic literature, interviews, and various digital platforms—including the use of emerging technologies such as Artificial Intelligence (AI) tools—for organizing and structuring content.

While every effort has been made to ensure the accuracy and authenticity of the information presented, the author does not accept any responsibility for errors, omissions, or any consequences arising from the use of this material. The views expressed are personal to the author and do not represent those of any organization, university, or government body unless specifically mentioned.

References to institutions, individuals, and programs are made in good faith and for illustrative or informational purposes only. The inclusion of such references does not imply any form of endorsement, affiliation, or criticism unless explicitly stated. Readers are advised to use their discretion and consult appropriate experts or official sources before drawing conclusions or making decisions based on this book.

This book is intended purely for educational and thought-leadership purposes and should not be construed as professional, legal, financial, or policy advice.

Copyright Notice

All rights reserved.

No part of this publication may be reproduced, stored in a retrieval system, or transmitted in any form or by any means—electronic, mechanical, photocopying, recording, scanning, or otherwise—without the prior written permission of the author, except in the case of brief quotations embodied in critical reviews and certain other non-commercial uses permitted by copyright law.

This book is protected under the Copyright Act of India and international copyright laws. Unauthorized reproduction, distribution, or transmission of any part of this work is strictly prohibited and may result in civil and criminal liability.

For rights, permissions, or collaboration inquiries, please contact:
ashishgupta.co.in | authorashishgupta@gmail.com

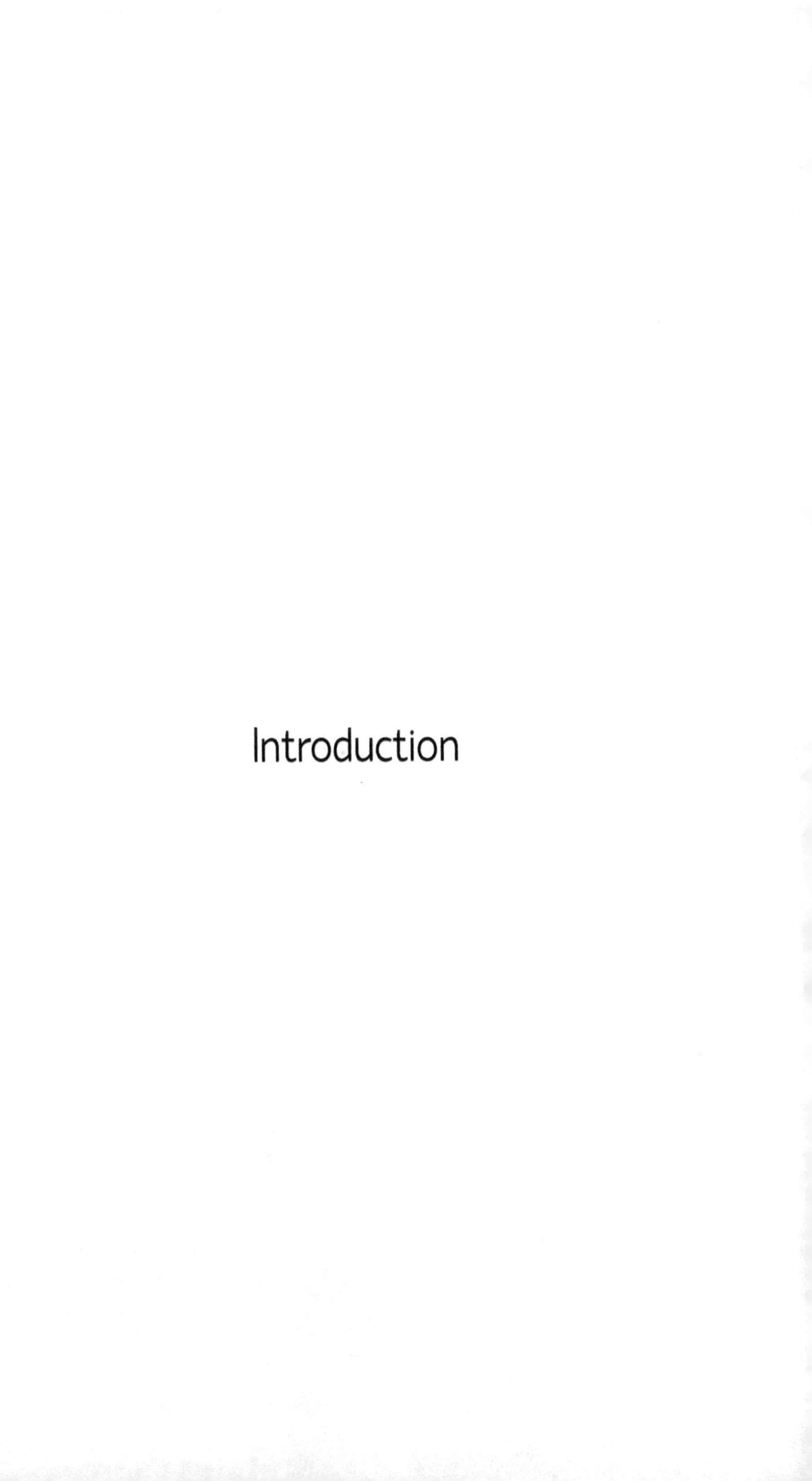

Introduction

CHAPTER ONE

Business Education as a Mirror of India's Economic Evolution

Business education in India has never existed in a vacuum. It has evolved in lockstep with the country's economic trajectory—shaped by shifts in policy, society, global influences, and the aspirations of a young, ambitious nation.

From the days of ancient trade routes and indigenous business models to the formalization of management principles in classrooms, the story of Indian business education is in many ways the story of India itself.

In the pre-colonial era, commerce was embedded in the fabric of Indian life. Merchant guilds (shrenis), joint family businesses, and indigenous accounting systems like bahi-khata and hundi reflected a sophisticated understanding of enterprise. These systems, while unwritten, were deeply ethical, community-driven, and sustainable.

Colonialism disrupted this native knowledge system. The British education model prioritized clerical training over entrepreneurial thinking, sidelining India's traditional business wisdom. The seeds of formal business education were sown in this period, but largely from a Western lens—focused on commerce rather than creativity, and compliance rather than innovation.

Post-independence, India's tryst with socialism demanded a new kind of business leader—one who could work within state-led planning, navigate bureaucracy, and still build institutions. The birth of the Indian Institutes of Management (IIMs) in the 1960s signaled the formal arrival of modern management education. These institutions were modeled on American business schools, blending global practices with local relevance. They became symbols of elite education, shaping a generation of professionals who would later lead India Inc.

Liberalization in 1991 was a turning point. As India opened its economy, the demand for business professionals exploded. The private sector stepped in to fill the gap, launching a wave of private B-schools, each promising employability, placement, and a shot at upward mobility. The rise of institutions like ISB, the focus on entrepreneurship, and the emergence of global collaborations reflected India's new economic confidence.

Today, we stand at another crossroads. The world is changing—digitally, environmentally, geopolitically. And once again, business schools must adapt. They must not just respond to market needs but anticipate them. They must move from being placement factories to becoming purpose-driven ecosystems that shape ethical, innovative, and resilient leaders.

This book explores this journey in depth—how business education has mirrored India's economic story, how it has influenced national growth, and how it must evolve to keep pace with the Bharat that is rising.

Because the future of Indian business education is not just about MBA rankings or campus placements—it is about nation-building.

CHAPTER TWO

From Gurukul to Global: A Contextual Overview

To fully understand the evolution of business education in India, one must zoom out and observe the cultural, historical, and philosophical shifts that have shaped learning in this land. India has always been a cradle of knowledge—its educational heritage far predates the idea of formal degrees, classrooms, or standardized curricula.

The Gurukul System: Learning Through Life - In ancient India, the Gurukul system was the earliest form of structured learning. Education was deeply personalized, value-driven, and holistic. While it is often associated with spiritual and philosophical teachings, Gurukuls also imparted knowledge about statecraft, agriculture, trade, accounting (Ganita), and ethical wealth management (Artha and Dharma). Business, in this era, was not just about profit—it was about duty, trust, and community well-being.

Merchants and traders were highly respected, and Indian cities like Varanasi, Ujjain, and Pataliputra were thriving hubs of trade and enterprise. The Arthashastra by Chanakya stands as a testament to the level of economic and managerial thinking present in ancient India. It discusses taxation, labor management, international trade, and even industrial espionage—topics that remain central to MBA classrooms today.

The Disruption of Colonization - The arrival of colonial rule brought a systematic dismantling of indigenous education and commerce. The British education system, particularly post-Macaulay's 1835 Minute, was designed to produce clerks and administrators rather than entrepreneurs or leaders. Traditional business acumen was seen as informal and unscientific, and English-language education took precedence over vernacular and value-based learning.

It was during this period that commerce colleges first emerged—in Mumbai, Calcutta, and Chennai. These early institutions focused on accounting, auditing, and trade regulations—geared more toward serving the British administrative machinery than building Indian business leadership.

Post-Independence Aspirations - After independence in 1947, India needed managerial talent to build institutions, industries, and infrastructure. The early IITs focused on science and technology, while business education remained limited to commerce streams. However, the founding of the Indian Institutes of Management (IIMs) in the 1960s marked a transformative moment. Inspired by the American model, these institutes offered rigorous programs based on case studies, quantitative methods, and strategic thinking.

The vision was to create professional managers who could lead the public and private sectors alike. With support from institutions like Harvard Business School and MIT Sloan, Indian management education began to take global shape, though still rooted in the post-socialist industrial reality of the country.

Liberalization and the Private Sector Boom - The economic liberalization of 1991 turned the tide once again. India moved from a state-driven to a market-driven economy. With this came a boom in private business schools, executive education, distance learning, and eventually, globally aligned models like the Indian School of Business (ISB).

As the economy opened up, so did education. Partnerships with foreign universities, executive MBA formats, international faculty, and cross-border case studies became common. A growing middle class saw the MBA as a passport to financial stability and social mobility.

The Global Future Rooted in Indian Wisdom - Today, Indian business education is at a juncture where it must be both global in outlook and Indian in spirit. As the world faces unprecedented disruptions—from climate change to AI, from geopolitical shifts to ethical capitalism—India's B-schools have the opportunity to redefine what it means to be a business leader.

Drawing from its ancient heritage, India can champion a model of business that is not just about shareholder value, but about human value. A model that respects dharma while embracing digital.

The journey from Gurukul to Global is not just geographical—it is philosophical. It is a journey from memorization to mindfulness, from imitation to innovation, from dependency to self-reliance.

This book is an attempt to chronicle that very journey.

Part I: The Origins

CHAPTER THREE

Roots of Commerce in Ancient India

Long before the modern notions of capitalism, corporate structures, or MBA classrooms emerged, India had already built a vibrant and deeply philosophical economic system. Trade, enterprise, and wealth creation were never merely commercial pursuits; they were expressions of dharma—righteousness, moral duty, and social responsibility. In ancient India, business was seamlessly woven into the spiritual, cultural, and societal fabric. It wasn't confined to profits or transactions; it was about creating harmony, stability, and prosperity for the larger community. Commerce was a path to service, not selfishness—a channel to achieve not just artha (wealth), but also dharma (duty), kama (desire), and ultimately moksha (liberation).

This foundational worldview shaped every aspect of economic life in Bharat. From ethical codes of conduct to guild-based entrepreneurship, from intellectual treatises to international trade, ancient India had laid down the principles of what we now call business strategy, governance, and sustainability. In fact, much of what is being discussed today in the global discourse on ethical capitalism, stakeholder theory, and sustainable business models was not only understood but practiced millennia ago in the Indian subcontinent.

The Shreni System: At the heart of this ancient business landscape were the shrenis—India's first trade guilds and arguably one of the earliest forms of organized corporate structure. A shreni was a professional guild formed by individuals engaged in a similar economic activity—such as weavers, blacksmiths, potters, merchants, or bankers. These guilds operated with remarkable autonomy, managing everything from quality control and training to dispute resolution and pricing norms. What made them unique was their deep integration with societal needs. They funded public works, supported education, built temples, and played a crucial role in local governance. Their influence extended far beyond commerce—they were agents of social good.

The shrenis were governed by internal councils and had their own set of ethical and operational codes. Entry into a shreni often required sponsorship, apprenticeship, and a commitment to uphold its values. Knowledge transfer was carried out through generations in a guru-shishya (mentor-disciple) model. This informal yet structured system of vocational education ensured both skill mastery and value orientation. In essence, these guilds were ancient India's answer to today's business federations, trade unions, and vocational training institutes—all rolled into one.

The role of the shrenis wasn't limited to domestic economics. Many of them were actively involved in international trade. Ancient Indian ports like Bharuch, Lothal, Kaveripattinam, and Tamralipti were buzzing centers of maritime commerce. Goods from India—textiles, spices, steel, ivory, gemstones—were highly sought after across Rome, Greece, Egypt, Southeast Asia, and China. Indian merchants established vast networks of trade, using caravans overland and ships across oceans. They developed sophisticated financial instruments like the hundi (a credit note akin to a modern bill of exchange) and kept records in traditional ledgers known as bahi-khatas.

THE SHRENI SYSTEM

INDIA'S FIRST BUSINESS GUILDS

Long before modern corporations, ancient India had shrenis—organized guilds of traders, artisans, and merchants. These were sophistictaed associations that operated like today's business federations. They managed:

 **Quality control of goods**

 **Regulation of wages and prices**

 **Arbitration of disputes**

 **Training of new members** (a precursor to vocational education)

 **Ethical business practices**

Despite this economic dynamism, business in ancient India was never seen in isolation from ethics. Most of these merchants were deeply spiritual, influenced by traditions like Jainism and Buddhism that emphasized simplicity, honesty, and compassion. Jain communities, in particular, became known for their frugality, discipline, and trust-based business practices. Profit was not shunned—but it was never pursued at the cost of societal or environmental well-being. In fact, one of the oldest ideas in Indian commerce was that true wealth is one that benefits many—not just the individual.

Arthashastra: Perhaps the most profound articulation of Indian economic thought came through the Arthashastra, written by the legendary strategist and scholar Kautilya (also known as Chanakya) around the 4th century BCE. Often compared to Machiavelli but far ahead of his time, Kautilya's Arthashastra is a masterclass in statecraft, economics, and organizational governance. It outlines principles of administration, trade policy, labor management, taxation, market regulation, corporate espionage, and even foreign relations. While it served as a manual for kings and administrators, its teachings remain incredibly relevant to today's business leaders.

The Arthashastra emphasized strategic thinking, efficient administration, and ethical governance. Kautilya argued that the prosperity of the state depended on its economic health, which in turn required a robust commercial ecosystem. He envisioned a system where state and private enterprises co-existed, where markets were regulated for fairness, and where the ultimate goal of economic activity was lok kalyan—the welfare of the people. He advocated for state-owned enterprises in critical sectors like mining, textiles, and shipping, but also encouraged private entrepreneurship under a watchful regulatory eye. His ideas on taxation—fair, proportionate, and incentive-based—sound strikingly modern in the era of tax reforms and ease-of-doing-business models.

ARTHASHASTRA:

THE WORLD'S FIRST TREATISE ON MANAGEMENT?

One of India's greatest contributions to economic thought is Kautilya's *Arthashastra* (circa 4th century BCE). Often dubbed India's Machiavelli, Kautilya was far ahead of his time. The *Arthashastra* covers:

 **Statecraft and taxation**

 **Labor management and industrial operations**

 **Trade policies and import-export systems**

 **Corporate espionage and competitor analysis**

 **Resource optimization and crisis planning**

Business and Economics in the Arthashastra

The Arthashastra outlines a robust vision of a state-managed but economically vibrant society, with the king as both a moral guardian and economic regulator. Some key business-related concepts include:

✔ Market Regulation

Establishment of a Superintent of Commerce to oversee trade, pricing, and merchant conduct
Setting price ceilings and preventing black marketing
Ensuring quality control and punishing fraud

✔ State Enterprises

Advocated for state-owned industries in key areas like mining, textiles, liquor, and shipping
Encouraged public-private partnerships, where state and private merchants co-invested in ventures

✔ Taxation & Revenue Management

Detailed and equitable taxation system based on income, produce, and trade
Encouraged productive enterprise over punitive taxation—similar to today's economic incentive models

✔ Trade & Foreign Relations

Emphasized the importance of foreign trade routes, import-export policies, and international diplomacy as economic tools

Kautilya was also a keen observer of human behavior and leadership. His insights into motivation, organization design, and crisis management mirror many frameworks taught in business schools today. He proposed performance-based rewards, detailed job descriptions, and accountability mechanisms. He warned against greed, nepotism, and incompetence—traits that, according to him, could destroy both the enterprise and the state. To him, leadership wasn't just about power; it was about purpose and prudence.

Indigenous Education System: Another remarkable feature of ancient Indian commerce was its indigenous education system. Although there were no formal "business schools," knowledge was passed through a blend of oral traditions, apprenticeship, family mentorship, and community discourse. Business wisdom was experiential, ethical, and deeply localized. Fathers trained sons, communities raised young apprentices, and elders served as repositories of time-tested strategies. This ensured not only the transmission of skills but also the preservation of cultural and ethical values associated with enterprise. The focus was on character, long-term reputation, and community trust—qualities that are being revisited today under the umbrella of leadership development and corporate social responsibility.

This deeply integrated model of commerce and culture, however, faced a steady decline with the onset of colonization. The British introduced a new system of education—rooted in English language and Western economic theories—that dismissed indigenous knowledge as archaic and unscientific. The traditional guilds were weakened, artisanal industries were disrupted, and Indian enterprises were systematically sidelined in favor of colonial monopolies. The narrative of Indian business was rewritten to suggest that modern enterprise came only with colonial intervention, ignoring centuries of thriving, ethical, and globally connected commerce.

Yet, this legacy isn't lost. It survives in the DNA of India's family-run businesses, in the cooperative movements like AMUL, in the frugal innovation of Indian entrepreneurs, and in the timeless values that continue to guide millions of traders, shopkeepers, and self-employed individuals across the country. And more importantly, it offers a powerful foundation upon which to reimagine business education in India today.

Understanding this history is not about romanticizing the past. It is about reconnecting with a worldview that can offer solutions to some of our most pressing modern problems—rising inequality, erosion of trust in corporations, environmental degradation, and unsustainable models of growth. When we speak today of ESG (Environmental, Social, and Governance) frameworks, inclusive capitalism, or stakeholder models of business, we are, in some sense, echoing the ancient Indian ethos of enterprise.

In the rush to emulate Western business models, we have often ignored our own. But now, as India rises again—economically, politically, and culturally—it is time to draw upon our indigenous intellectual and ethical heritage. It is time to recognize that India's tryst with business education did not begin in 1961 with the establishment of the first Indian Institutes of Management. It began much earlier—in the pages of the Arthashastra, in the ledgers of the shrenis, in the ports of Bharuch, and in the bazaars of Ujjain. It began in Bharat, centuries ago.

As this book will go on to explore, the journey of business education in India has been a fascinating tale of interruption, adaptation, and rediscovery. But to truly understand where we are going, we must understand where we started. And we started not with case studies or KPIs, but with karma, community, and dharma. The real legacy of Indian business lies not in quarterly reports, but in centuries of wisdom that taught us how to build enterprises that are not only profitable but also purposeful.

In reclaiming this legacy, we don't just honor our past—we equip ourselves to shape a more balanced, ethical, and sustainable future.

The B-school journey, then, is not merely an academic one. It is civilizational. And it begins here.

Colonial Influence in Education

The story of India's business education cannot be told without examining the tectonic shift that occurred during British colonial rule. The colonization of India was not merely a political conquest; it was an intellectual disruption. It rewired the nation's knowledge systems, diluted its indigenous strengths, and redefined the purpose of education from one of civilizational growth to one of administrative convenience. For centuries, India had nurtured its own rich traditions of commerce, leadership, and learning—systems that evolved through communities, guilds, oral traditions, and spiritual frameworks. But with the arrival of British power, education was weaponized. It was no longer a tool for self-realization or societal advancement—it became an instrument of control.

Macaulay's Minute: The Turning Point - The most defining moment in this disruption came in 1835 with Lord Thomas Babington Macaulay's infamous "Minute on Indian Education." With one sweeping proclamation, Macaulay dismissed India's ancient wisdom as inferior to European thought, stating that "a single shelf of a good European library is worth the whole native literature of India and Arabia." He proposed that India abandon its centuries-old languages of knowledge—Sanskrit and Persian—in favor of English. Funding for traditional institutions like Madrasas,

Gurukuls, and Pathshalas was withdrawn. In their place, British-style schools began to emerge, designed not to foster independent thinking or enterprise, but to create a class of educated Indians who were "Indian in blood and colour, but English in taste, in opinions, in morals, and in intellect." These individuals would serve as clerks and intermediaries for the British administration, not as leaders of an independent economy or society.

This reorientation of education was especially damaging to India's business traditions. For centuries, Indian commerce had thrived on oral knowledge, community-based mentoring, apprenticeship, and spiritual grounding. Business was not a separate subject—it was part of life, often learned in the family firm, the temple courtyard, or the bustling bazaar. The values of trust, sustainability, and long-term thinking guided business practices. Yet, in the new colonial education system, such knowledge was deemed "unscientific" and systematically sidelined. Commerce entered the curriculum, but only in a narrow and bureaucratic form. Students were taught how to maintain ledgers, conduct audits, and perform basic economic analysis—but not how to build or lead a business.

From Merchants to Clerks: The Framing of Commerce - The focus was on creating efficient clerical workers, not on cultivating independent entrepreneurs. Indian trade history, entrepreneurial practices, and indigenous economic models were absent from textbooks. There was no room for the study of traditional systems like the hundi (early banking instruments), bahi-khata (native accounting), or the shrenis (guilds). Business education, under colonial influence, was reduced to a means of employment, not empowerment.

Macaulay's Minute:
The Turning Point

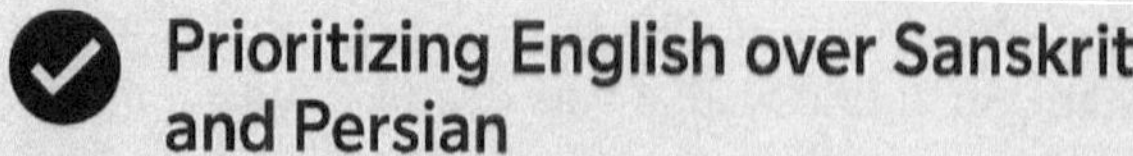

"A *single shelf of* a good European library is worth the whole native literature of India and Arabia."

With this sweeping—and deeply colonial—statement, he argued for:

- ✓ Prioritizing English over Sanskrit and Persian

- ✓ Promoting European science, history, and literature

- ✓ Training Indians to be "interpreters between us and the millions whom we govern"

- ✓ Replacing indigenous educational institutions with Anglicized, classroom-based learning

The resulting model aimed to produce a class of educated Indians who would be loyal, literate, and administratively useful—but not economically independent or entrepreneurial.

NEGLECT OF COMMERCE AND ENTREPRENEURSHIP

One of the most glaring absences in Macaulay's vision was the exclusion of commerce, trade, and practical economics from the curriculum. The impact was severe:

Traditional business knowledge—like bahi-khata systems, hundi transactions, and community-led trade models—was labeled "unscientific" and sidelined.

No structured education was provided in business skills, trade ethics, or entrepreneurial thinking.

Commerce was reduced to accounting and bookkeeping, aimred at fulfilling roles in British-run trading firms, not Indian-owned enterprises.

Vocational learning and apprenticeships, once passed down through quilds (shrenis) and families, were discouraged in favor of rote learning

The British educational system in India created employees, not entrepreneurs—servants of the empire, not creators of independent enterprise.

Despite this systemic suppression, certain commerce-focused institutions did emerge during the British era. The most prominent among them was Sydenham College of Commerce and Economics, established in Mumbai in 1913. It was the first dedicated commerce college in India, aimed at training Indians to work in commercial roles within British-run companies and banks. The college offered structured education in subjects like accounting, economics, business law, and auditing, all aligned with British regulations. Around the same time, colleges like Presidency College in Calcutta, the College of Commerce in Lahore, and Delhi College of Commerce (which would later evolve into Shri Ram College of Commerce) began offering commerce courses. These institutions laid the foundational structure of business education in India, but their intent was colonial. They focused on producing manpower for the colonial economy rather than visionaries for Indian enterprise.

While these colleges provided technical skills, they did little to inspire innovation, leadership, or entrepreneurship. The curriculum was heavily theoretical and Eurocentric. It taught Adam Smith, Ricardo, and Keynes, but ignored Kautilya's Arthashastra or India's ancient trade systems. It trained students to be subordinates in foreign-led firms, not founders of their own ventures. There was no space for strategy, vision, or creativity. Even the pedagogy was didactic—rote memorization replaced discussion; conformity replaced questioning. The spirit of enterprise was missing. These institutions were not business schools in the truest sense—they were training centers for compliance and conformity.

Impact of Indian Business Communities: The true story of Indian business education during the colonial period, however, is incomplete without acknowledging the role of India's resilient business communities. Marwaris, Banias, Jains, Chettiars, and Parsis continued to educate their children in parallel systems—through family businesses, community mentoring, and hands-on apprenticeship. While colonial institutions trained clerks, these communities trained entrepreneurs. Children learned mental math by managing shop accounts, learned ethics by watching elders resolve disputes, and developed negotiation skills in the marketplace—not the classroom. They internalized a code of conduct that blended profitability with purpose, and tradition with innovation. In many cases, these communities sent their children to commerce colleges to acquire formal certification but never relied solely on them for practical education. The classroom was secondary; the shop floor was primary.

The duality of this learning system—colonial education on one hand and indigenous mentoring on the other—shaped the Indian business landscape for much of the late 19th and early 20th centuries. Yet, it also created a paradox. While Indian businesses adapted to survive, they often did so without institutional recognition or support. The British did not see Indian entrepreneurship as worthy of celebration or academic study. Instead, they viewed it with suspicion or indifference. Indigenous business practices were never documented, codified, or validated in formal education. This created a generational gap in confidence—a sense that Indian models were somehow inferior or "informal," even though they were deeply effective.

Seeds of Reform & Resistance: Amid this environment, there were also voices of resistance—visionaries who saw the need to reclaim education as a tool for national development. Leaders like Dadabhai Naoroji, Mahatma Gandhi, and Rabindranath Tagore questioned the colonial model and advocated for systems that reflected Indian realities. Gandhi's idea of Nai Talim, or Basic Education, emphasized hands-on work, self-reliance, and moral development. He believed that true education should cultivate dignity of labor and connection to one's roots. While Nai Talim was not a business curriculum per se, its spirit was entrepreneurial. It encouraged making, building, and creating—values essential to any economy. Rabindranath Tagore, through his institution Visva-Bharati, attempted to integrate Indian culture, art, and enterprise into the learning process. These reform efforts were limited in institutional reach but profound in philosophical impact. They planted the seeds for post-independence educational reform.

THE COLLAPSE OF INDIGENOUS INSTITUTIONS

Alongside the imposition of Macaulay's system came the gradual erosion of India's indigenous education and business institutions:

Thousands of pathshalas, madrasas, gurukuls, and artisan training centers were defunded or dismantled

The merchant guild system declined as trade became centralized under British control

Indian communities that had historically been economic powerhouses—like Marwaris, Chettiars, and Parsis—were now forced to adapt their business acumen outside tre formal education system

Commerce, once viewed as a dharmic pursuit, was now reframed as subordinate Labor under the British East India Company

The long-term consequence of colonial education was a generation of Indians conditioned to aspire for government jobs and salaried security, rather than venture into risk-taking or wealth creation. Commerce was respected as a subject, but only in the context of job readiness. The idea that one could build a business—let alone change the world through enterprise—was absent from the mainstream narrative. The psychological impact was perhaps deeper than the structural one. A society that once saw business as a dharmic pursuit, a way to serve society, began to view it with suspicion or inferiority. The entrepreneur became the outsider, while the bureaucrat became the model citizen.

Yet, out of this disruption came the recognition that India needed its own educational renaissance—one that would undo the intellectual damage of colonial rule and rekindle the spirit of enterprise that had once defined the nation. The independence movement itself was not just political—it was also educational. It was a struggle to reclaim the right to think, to build, and to lead. With freedom came the possibility of designing institutions that served Indian needs, values, and ambitions. The birth of the Indian Institutes of Management in the 1960s was not just a milestone in business education—it was a civilizational response to colonial disruption.

As we move into the next chapters of this journey, we will see how India began to redefine business education in its own image. But to appreciate that transformation, we must fully grasp the legacy it sought to overcome—a legacy of educational dependency, economic subservience, and intellectual suppression. The colonial system gave India schools and colleges, but it took away confidence, context, and continuity. It taught us how to follow rules but not how to break new ground. It produced accountants, not architects of change. And yet, through resilience, reform, and the enduring spirit of enterprise, India would find its way back.

The B-School Saga, then, is not just a story of institutions—it is the story of a civilization reclaiming its agency. The British may have disrupted the flow of Indian commerce and business education, but they could not erase its roots. Those roots lay deep—in the markets of Gujarat, the guilds of Tamil Nadu, the merchant ships of Kerala, and the ledgers of Rajasthan. And from those roots, new shoots would emerge—shaped by modernity, but grounded in memory. The age of Indian business schools was about to begin.

CHAPTER FIVE

Birth of Indian Business Schools

Laying the Foundation for Managerial India: As India inched closer to independence in the mid-20th century, the national imagination turned not just toward political self-rule, but economic self-reliance. The vision was clear: an India that would be built by its own hands, led by its own minds. To achieve this, the country needed more than idealism—it needed planning, execution, and professionalism. This wasn't just a job for engineers and scientists; it called for managers—individuals who could lead institutions, build organizations, and transform blueprints into functioning systems. In this context, the seeds of India's business education movement were sown—not as a market response to corporate demand, but as a moral and intellectual response to the call for nation-building. The first Indian business schools were not born in gleaming towers with global rankings in mind; they began as humble, often government-supported efforts to infuse managerial thinking into a newly independent nation.

IISWBM: The Pioneer in Management Education - The pioneering institution that marked the dawn of formal business education in India was the Indian Institute of Social Welfare and Business Management (IISWBM), established in 1953 in Kolkata. It was the first business school in independent India, and one of the earliest in Asia. Its origins were unique—it was not merely an academic experiment but a collaboration between the University of Calcutta and the Ministry of Rehabilitation. The timing was significant: the post-Partition rehabilitation efforts required structured administration and human resource management. The institute's vision reflected this need—it aimed not only to teach business administration but to cultivate professionals who could lead both governmental and industrial organizations with compassion and competence. The curriculum focused on areas like Social Welfare Administration, Industrial Relations, Personnel Management, and Labour Welfare—subjects that mirrored the nation's priorities in the aftermath of colonial rule and social upheaval.

IISWBM's approach was broad and inclusive. It understood that management was not just about profits and spreadsheets—it was also about people, systems, and public good. Long before the rise of Human Resource Management as a discipline, IISWBM introduced Indian students to the world of labor laws, industrial psychology, organizational behavior, and social enterprise. Its training programs were designed for those who would go on to lead public sector undertakings (PSUs), state welfare departments, cooperatives, and labor unions.

The idea was to blend the best of administrative efficiency with a strong ethical compass. Located in Kolkata—a city with a legacy of industrialization, intellectualism, and reform—the institute naturally became a center for thought and practice. Though its name doesn't always feature in today's headlines, IISWBM laid a foundational stone for India's business education landscape, nurturing professionals who believed that management was, above all, a service to society.

The Indian Institute of Social Welfare and Business Management (IISWBM), established in 1953 in Kolkata, is widely regarded as India's first official business school.

Born out of a collaboration between the University of Calcutta and the Ministry of Rehabilitation, IISWBM began by offering programs in social welfare and personnal management—areas that reflected the nation-building priorities of that era

Its emphasis was on producing socially conscious managers who could work in both government and industry 

While it didn't attract national attention like the IIMs would later, IISWBM laid the groundwork for structured management education in India

Parallel to this pioneering effort, India already had a number of commerce colleges in operation, particularly in cities like Mumbai, Delhi, and Chennai. These institutions—though not business schools in the modern MBA sense—played a vital role in introducing structured commerce education to Indian students. Sydenham College of Commerce and Economics, established in 1913 in Mumbai, was the first of its kind. It offered courses in accounting, business law, economics, and finance, producing generations of skilled accountants, clerks, and junior executives who would serve in banks, insurance firms, and trading companies. Similarly, Presidency College in Kolkata and Delhi College of Commerce (later renamed Shri Ram College of Commerce, or SRCC) contributed significantly to building the academic scaffolding for commerce education. While these institutions lacked the strategic and leadership focus that business schools would later bring, they created a pipeline of commercially literate professionals and legitimized business-related studies within the Indian academic ecosystem.

The Planning Comission and the Demand for Managers: By the late 1940s and early 1950s, as India adopted a mixed economy model and began rolling out its Five-Year Plans, the need for managerial talent became even more acute. The Planning Commission, under economists like P.C. Mahalanobis, recognized that India's vision of rapid industrialization and public sector-led development could not be executed without a cadre of trained managers. These were not managers in the corporate sense alone—but professionals who could lead large-scale projects, manage state-run enterprises, streamline government departments, and handle complex logistical challenges in a resource-starved economy. The role of a manager, in this context, was part technocrat, part administrator, part visionary. India needed leadership that could translate policy into practice—not just in boardrooms, but on factory floors, in irrigation projects, in rural cooperatives, and in urban planning commissions.

Post-1947, as India adopted a mixed economy model and launched Five-Year Plans, the government realized that running state enterprises and public sector units required trained managerial talent. The Planning Commission, under the leadership of visionaries like P.C. Mahalanobois, emphasized the need for:

Trained professionals to manage industrial projects

Leadership for the public sector

Scientific approaches to administration and policy execution

This realization triggered an important shift in India's education policy. It was no longer enough to teach commerce or accountancy in undergraduate colleges. What India needed was institutions dedicated to advanced, postgraduate-level management education—institutes that could create leaders, strategists, and institution-builders. Around this time, Indian policymakers and intellectuals began looking abroad for models to emulate. The American business school system, especially Harvard Business School and MIT Sloan, attracted significant attention. Their emphasis on case-based learning, decision sciences, organizational behavior, and strategic thinking was seen as highly relevant. Indian educationists, along with international development agencies like the Ford Foundation and Harvard Business School faculty, began to collaborate with Indian government officials to explore the creation of elite management institutes in India. These discussions would eventually lead to the establishment of the Indian Institutes of Management (IIMs), beginning in the early 1960s.

The Pioneers: Visionaries Who Saw the Future - who However, before the IIMs rose to national prominence, it was individuals like Professor D.K. Desai and Vikram Sarabhai who provided intellectual leadership for management education in India. Desai, a professor at the University of Bombay, was one of the first to advocate for scientific management in India and called for the integration of economic planning with organizational efficiency. Sarabhai, widely regarded as the father of India's space program, believed that management was not merely a corporate function but a national necessity. His vision led to the establishment of IIM Ahmedabad in collaboration with Harvard Business School. Dr. Bidhan Chandra Roy, the then Chief Minister of West Bengal and a strong advocate of developmental planning, also played a key role in supporting IISWBM's foundation. These visionaries were not businessmen—they were scientists, economists, and reformers who believed in the transformative power of structured management education.

At the same time, other cities across India were building their own regional centers of excellence. Mumbai, as the commercial capital, had a head start with institutions like Sydenham and, later, the Jamnalal Bajaj Institute of Management Studies (JBIMS), established in 1965. JBIMS, often referred to as the 'CEO Factory,' became known for producing corporate leaders, especially in finance and marketing. Its proximity to India's banking and financial ecosystem gave it a unique industry interface. In Delhi, the Faculty of Management Studies (FMS) was established under Delhi University in 1954, offering one of the earliest full-time MBA programs in India.

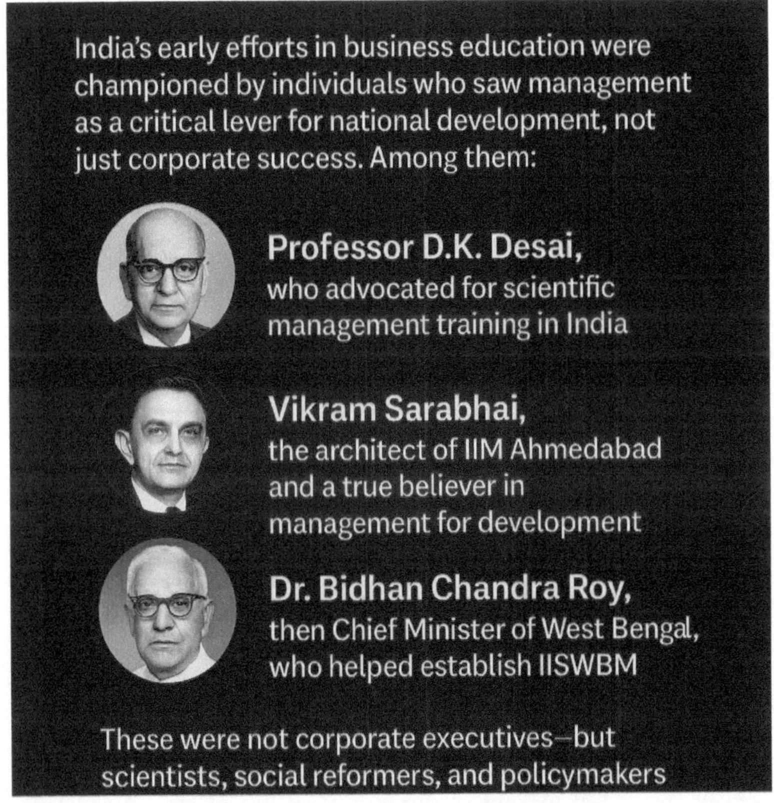

FMS combined academic rigor with cost-effective education, maintaining a strong focus on public service and ethics. In Chennai, Loyola College had already built a reputation for excellence in commerce, which eventually led to the establishment of the Loyola Institute of Business Administration (LIBA) in 1979—a business school with Jesuit values emphasizing service, ethics, and leadership.

These regional institutions, while operating independently of each other, collectively laid the intellectual and institutional foundation for India's management education culture. They brought credibility to business as an academic discipline, attracted faculty from economics, psychology, sociology, and engineering, and introduced Indian students to the interdisciplinary nature of management. They helped Indian families overcome the colonial stigma that commerce was inferior to law, medicine, or civil services. For a generation of students who once dreamed only of becoming IAS officers or doctors, business schools opened up a new horizon—a path of professional excellence, organizational leadership, and societal impact.

In retrospect, what stands out about these early business schools is their clarity of purpose. They were not driven by market demand or global rankings, but by a nationalistic vision. They saw management not as a tool for profit maximization, but as a skill set essential to building a new India. They trained people to run factories, administer labor laws, launch development schemes, and reform public institutions. Their graduates entered not only corporations but also cooperatives, NGOs, government departments, and academic institutions. This broad social footprint gave early business education in India a unique character—one that was deeply aligned with the ideals of independence, development, and social justice.

The birth of Indian business schools, therefore, cannot be understood in isolation from the birth of modern India itself. These schools were not merely academic institutions; they were nation-building laboratories. They arose from a conviction that if India were to grow economically, it needed to think scientifically, act strategically, and manage professionally. Management education in India did not begin with the intent to chase capitalism; it began with the intent to create capacity. That intent, as we shall see in the chapters ahead, would evolve, expand, and occasionally be challenged—but its origins remain firmly rooted in the vision of a self-reliant Bharat.

The emergence of IISWBM, SRCC, Sydenham, FMS, and JBIMS marked the beginning of a journey. What followed next would be a giant leap—a move from regional excellence to national prominence, from managerial training to global benchmarking. The rise of the Indian Institutes of Management was not just a milestone—it was a movement.

Part II: The Rise of the IIMs

CHAPTER SIX

The Visionaries Behind IIMs

How a Bold Vision Gave Birth to India's Premier Management Institutions: The 1960s were a watershed decade for India—a young republic standing at the crossroads of aspiration and execution. Having broken free from colonial rule just over a decade earlier, India was in the throes of planning its future. The vision was clear: a self-reliant economy driven by industrial development, robust public sector enterprises, and equitable growth. But that vision needed more than policies and infrastructure; it required human capital—capable leaders and professional managers who could convert development blueprints into functioning realities. The country had engineers and scientists trained at newly established institutions like the IITs. What it needed next was a new kind of professional—the manager. This urgent demand gave rise to a bold experiment in education and institution-building. And at the center of it stood a group of visionary leaders who imagined, shaped, and delivered what would become India's most iconic educational institutions: the Indian Institutes of Management.

The seeds of the IIMs were sown not in business lobbies or global think tanks, but in the fertile minds of Indian statesmen, scientists, economists, and social reformers who believed in institution-building as a tool for nation-building. At the helm of this movement was India's first Prime Minister, Jawaharlal Nehru. Known for his love of science and his faith in rationality, Nehru was the architect of modern India's institutional architecture. Under his leadership, the country witnessed the establishment of the Planning Commission, the IITs, and a host of public sector enterprises. Nehru believed deeply in creating institutions that could generate intellectual capacity, innovation, and administrative excellence. He recognized early on that economic growth would require more than machines—it would require minds that could lead with discipline, vision, and purpose. His political endorsement and strategic backing played a vital role in the conception and birth of the IIMs.

If Nehru was the political force behind the IIMs, Dr. Vikram Sarabhai was the philosophical and institutional architect. A physicist and the driving force behind India's space program, Sarabhai viewed management as a discipline that extended far beyond the walls of corporate boardrooms. To him, it was a tool for societal transformation. Sarabhai envisioned a new India that needed professionals trained not just in technical know-how but in the ability to lead change, coordinate resources, and manage complexity.

With this conviction, he spearheaded the establishment of IIM Ahmedabad in 1961. His approach was radical for its time—he believed in academic freedom, autonomy from bureaucratic control, and a curriculum that balanced global standards with Indian realities. His partnership with Harvard Business School ensured that IIM Ahmedabad was built on the case method, a pedagogy that emphasized critical thinking, real-world problem-solving, and participative learning.

Ravi Matthai: Building a Distinctive Indian Model

Ravi J. Matthai, the first full-time Director of IIM Ahmedabad, brought a new level of integrity, independence, and Indian-ness to the institution.

A brilliant academic with degrees from Oxford and experience in the corporate world, Matthai believed IIMs should not be clones of their Western counterparts.

He pioneered the "Facuity Development Model" and promoted autonomy in governance, ensuring that IIMs remained intellectually independent and committed to India's unique challenges.

Matthai also initiated the **Jawaja Project** in Rajasthan—an effort to apply management principles to rural development.

This underscored a critical point: management was not just for boardrooms, but also for villages.

Matthai also initiated the Jawaja Project in Rajasthan—an effort to apply management principles to rural development

Ravi Matthai: Building a Distinctive Indian Model - But the IIM story wasn't just about infrastructure or pedagogy—it was about people. Among the most significant figures in this narrative was Ravi J. Matthai, the first full-time director of IIM Ahmedabad. A brilliant academic and former corporate executive, Matthai was a rare combination of idealism and pragmatism. He took Sarabhai's vision and turned it into a lived institutional culture. Matthai introduced a faculty governance model that preserved intellectual independence and shielded the institution from political interference.

He also believed that management education should serve not only industry but also society. His most profound contribution was the Jawaja Project in rural Rajasthan—an experiment in applying management principles to empower local artisans and communities. Through this project, Matthai underscored a powerful message: that management could—and should—be used for grassroots transformation, not just corporate success.

Parallelly, IIM Calcutta was taking shape on the eastern coast, with a slightly different but equally influential legacy. Its founding director, Dr. K.T. Chandy, brought a strong corporate perspective, having served as chairman of Hindustan Lever. Under his leadership, IIM Calcutta established a partnership with MIT Sloan School of Management. This collaboration gave the institute a distinct academic orientation focused on quantitative methods, systems thinking, and data-driven decision-making. The involvement of MIT and the Ford Foundation in shaping the curriculum, training faculty, and advising on governance models ensured that IIM Calcutta became a beacon of analytical rigor in management education.

The Ford Foundation and International Collaborations

The establishment of IIMs was not just a domestic effort—it was the result of global collaboration. The Indian government, under Nehru's leadership, sought assistance from the Ford Foundation, a U.S.-based philanthropic organization.

- Funding early infrastructure and faculty development

- Facilitating academic partnerships with Harvard Business School (for IIM Calcutta) and MIT Sloan School of Management (for IIM Ahmedabad)

- Introducing the case study method and experiential learning models to Indian classrooms

- Introducing the case study method and experiential learning models to Indian classrooms

The Ford Foundation and International Collaborations: The role of the Ford Foundation in this journey cannot be overstated. As a bridge between Indian aspirations and American academic expertise, the Foundation funded early infrastructure, enabled faculty exchanges, and facilitated curriculum development. It was through their initiative that Harvard and MIT became knowledge partners to IIMA and IIMC respectively. Harvard introduced the case study method, mentored Indian faculty, and helped establish the governance and pedagogy frameworks for IIMA. MIT, on the other hand, brought in its analytical and systems orientation to IIM Calcutta, reinforcing the role of management science in decision-making. This East-West collaboration became one of the most successful knowledge partnerships in postcolonial education history. It ensured that Indian business schools began not with inferiority complexes but with confidence, drawing from the best in the world while remaining rooted in Indian needs.

As the first batch of students entered these campuses, the institutions already bore a distinct identity—autonomous, rigorous, and mission-driven. The IIMs were designed as faculty-led institutions, where professors were not mere employees but stakeholders in the school's evolution. The curriculum focused equally on private sector dynamics and public sector management. The admission process emphasized merit, with a standardized entrance exam that would later evolve into the CAT (Common Admission Test). Most significantly, the IIMs rejected the conventional Indian university model in favor of autonomy and academic freedom. They weren't subservient to state boards or ministries; they were governed by independent boards that included industry leaders, academics, and policymakers.

This blend of autonomy, excellence, and social responsibility made the IIMs stand apart from day one. They were not clones of Western schools but uniquely Indian institutions with a global outlook. They trained managers who could work across sectors—whether in steel plants or banks, NGOs or government departments, MNCs or state cooperatives. This breadth of application was made possible by the vision of early contributors like Professor Samuel Paul, who emphasized public systems management during his tenure at IIM Bangalore. His belief that governance and public administration should be part of management education expanded the horizons of Indian B-schools.

Importantly, the IIMs were not born out of market demand. They were a response to national necessity. Their early years were not characterized by glamorous placements or global rankings but by a deep commitment to building a new India. Students were expected not only to become efficient executives but responsible citizens. The narrative was not about personal success, but national service. And in that lies the enduring ethos of the IIMs: they were never just about getting a job—they were about shaping a generation.

Over the years, as India liberalized and the private sector boomed, the IIMs evolved to meet the needs of a changing economy. But the DNA of these institutions—their commitment to excellence, ethics, and relevance—remained intact. That DNA was shaped in the 1960s by visionaries who thought beyond the immediate, who believed that education was not a commodity, but a cornerstone of nation-building.

In conclusion, the birth of the IIMs was not an administrative decision—it was a dream, fueled by purpose, and executed with precision. It brought together politics, academia, philanthropy, and global collaboration in one of the most ambitious educational ventures of modern India. Thanks to Nehru's institutional foresight, Sarabhai's intellectual leadership, Matthai's idealistic pragmatism, and the international partnerships that supported them, India created not just business schools—but leadership laboratories for a developing world. In the chapters ahead, we will see how these institutions evolved in the decades that followed, becoming symbols of aspiration, excellence, and national pride.

CHAPTER SEVEN

The Founding Years: IIM Ahmedabad and IIM Calcutta

Building India's Management Powerhouses: The year 1961 marked a defining moment in India's educational and economic journey. As the country took its first confident strides into the second decade of independence, two institutions were quietly but powerfully reshaping the way India would prepare its leaders for the future. These were the Indian Institutes of Management—Calcutta and Ahmedabad—born out of a shared national aspiration to create a generation of professional managers who could steward India's development. Though founded around the same time, these two institutes evolved with distinctly different academic influences, pedagogical models, and institutional cultures. Yet, at their core, they embodied the same purpose: to enable India to manage complexity with competence, and to align leadership with national service.

IIM Calcutta (IIMC), the first to be established, came into being through a collaborative venture between the Government of India, the Ford Foundation, and the Sloan School of Management at the Massachusetts Institute of Technology (MIT). The intellectual DNA of IIMC was built around systems thinking, quantitative rigor, and analytical problem-solving. In a country largely new to structured management education, this was a revolutionary shift. Early faculty members, many trained at MIT or mentored by visiting American professors, brought with them a scientific mindset and a penchant for data-driven decision-making. Operations research, statistics, econometrics, and computational thinking became core pillars of the IIMC curriculum. Even in the pre-digital age, IIM Calcutta introduced computers into learning environments, positioning itself as a technologically forward institute long before such practices became mainstream.

From its initial location at the historic Emerald Bower campus in north Kolkata to its eventual move to a sprawling facility in Joka, IIM Calcutta built a legacy of academic excellence, intellectual inquiry, and public policy engagement. Its early graduates entered a variety of fields—consulting, government services, development administration, and the nascent private sector—bringing a rigorously analytical lens to leadership. The institute earned a reputation for producing professionals who were as comfortable modeling economic behavior as they were designing organizational strategy. IIMC's early years were not glamorous, but they were transformative. They proved that India could absorb and internalize global knowledge while creating contextually rooted leadership.

Across the country in Ahmedabad, another experiment was unfolding—equally bold, yet fundamentally different in philosophy and approach. IIM Ahmedabad (IIMA) was the brainchild of Dr. Vikram Sarabhai, the brilliant physicist who also led India's space program. Sarabhai envisioned management education not merely as a tool for business efficiency, but as a vehicle for social transformation. His goal was to produce leaders who could serve society, not just industry. To realize this, he brought in Harvard Business School as the institutional partner. Unlike MIT's systems approach, Harvard introduced IIMA to the case method—a participatory pedagogy where students learned by discussing real-world problems, challenging assumptions, and defending decisions.

IIM Calcutta: India's First IIM

IIM Calcutta (IIMC) holds the distinction of being India's first Indian Institute of Management.

Established through a collaboration between the Government of India, the Ford Foundation, and th Sloan School of Management at MIT, IIM Calcutta was rooted in the belief that India needed professional managers trained with analytical, scientific, and systems-based thinking.

Key Highlights of IIMC's Early Years:

- Strong emphasis on quantitative methods, operations research, and systems analysis—heavily influenced by MIT.

- The use of computers and management science in decision-making was introduced early, making it the more technically orfented IIM at the fime.

- Faculty support and training were provided by international professors and Indian experts alike, leading to a rapid infusion of global academic culture

- Initially located at the Emerald Bower campus in north Kolkata before moving to Joka, Its permanent home.

IIM Calcutta quickly gained a reputation for producing sharp, analytical minds, many of whom went on to become economists, consultants, civil servants, and industry leaders.

At the heart of IIMA's development was Ravi J. Matthai, the first full-time director, whose tenure shaped the institute's ethos. Matthai emphasized academic autonomy, faculty-driven governance, and relevance to Indian challenges. He believed that management was as much about values as it was about valuation. Under his leadership, IIMA pioneered experiments like the Jawaja Project—a rural development initiative that applied management thinking to empower artisans and marginalized communities in Rajasthan. These efforts were not peripheral; they were central to IIMA's mission of building a management philosophy suited for a developing, democratic, and diverse nation.

The academic structure of IIMA reflected its collaborative roots with Harvard. The case study method became its pedagogical backbone, fostering critical thinking, collaborative learning, and context-specific decision-making. Faculty played a central role in institutional governance, curriculum development, and research direction. Students were treated not as passive recipients of knowledge but as active participants in a learning ecosystem. The IIMA campus, designed by the legendary American architect Louis Kahn, was more than a set of buildings—it was a visual metaphor for the institute's identity: modern, open, and timeless.

Though united in their commitment to excellence, IIMA and IIMC were shaped by their unique international partnerships. IIMC's connection with MIT Sloan imbued it with a quantitative, systems-oriented outlook. It became known for its strength in areas like operations research, logistics, decision science, and mathematical modeling. IIMA, influenced by Harvard, developed a problem-solving, leadership-focused culture that prioritized field immersion, social impact, and organizational behavior. The contrasting influences created two complementary centers of excellence—one technical and analytical, the other strategic and values-driven. Together, they demonstrated that India did not have to choose a single path to modernity—it could walk many.

IIM Ahmedabad: The Vision of Purpose-Driven Management

While IIMC.was being shaped in the east, a powerful experiment in the west was taoking shape–IIMA ⋀Бda: Spearheadoy Dr. Vikrarn Sarabhai, IIMA·'s foundation was rooted in an entirely different yet complementary philosophy; management as a force for societal transformation.

Sarabhai, with support from Dr. Jivraj Mehta ('then Chief Minister of Gujarat), end collaboration from Harvard Business School, envisioned IIMA as a crucibule for ethical, entrepreneurial, socially responsible le-dership.

Distinctive Features of IIMA's Foundation:

- Case **study method imported** from Harvard was central to the **pedagogy**, Students leamed through real-world problem-solving, not just theoretical instruction.

- A **strong faculty** governance model ensured academic freedom and institutional autonomy.

- Early leaders like Ravi J. Matthai, the first full-time Director, institutionalized the philosophy of "excellence with relevance." **emphas**zing Indian problems, Indian solutions, Indian solutions.

- IIMA consciously embraced challenges beyond corporate boardrooms–contributing to rural development, public systems, and cooperative mariagement (e.g. AMUL and IRMA collaborations).

The Harvard vs. MIT Influence: Two Distinct Cultures

While both IIMs shared common goals, their academic DNA reflected their founding collaborations:

Aspect	IIM Calcutta	IIM Ahmedabad
International Partner	MIT Sloan	Harvard Business School
Academic Emphasis	Quantitative Techniques & Systems	Case Study Method & Decision-Making
Orientation	Analytical & Research-Oriented	Practice-Based & Problem-Solving
Initial Strength	Technology, Modeling, OR	Strategy, Leadership, Rural Engagement

Both institutions faced formidable challenges in their formative years. Faculty recruitment was a persistent struggle, as India had few professionals trained in modern management principles. Many early educators came from backgrounds in economics, psychology, engineering, or public administration, and had to retrain themselves in emerging business disciplines. Infrastructure was basic, and in many cases, borrowed—campuses were temporary, libraries understocked, and classrooms modest. Skepticism from industry and government alike posed additional hurdles; "MBA" was not yet a term of prestige in India, and employers were unsure how to integrate these new graduates into existing hierarchies.

Yet, the visionaries behind these institutions were relentless. They focused not on what was lacking, but on what could be built. The Ford Foundation, in particular, played a crucial role by providing funding, facilitating international partnerships, and encouraging research and experimentation. Professors from Harvard and MIT trained Indian faculty, co-created curricula, and introduced new pedagogical methods. The goal was not to transplant Western institutions but to adapt their best features into the Indian context. And that's precisely what happened. Over time, Indian case studies replaced Western ones. Courses were tailored to local governance challenges, cooperative movements, and public sector needs. Summer internships with Indian companies and government departments became integral to the curriculum, ensuring that students remained grounded in Indian realities.

The two-year Post Graduate Programme (PGP) became the flagship offering at both IIMA and IIMC. The first-year curriculum focused on foundational courses—accounting, economics, statistics, organizational behavior, marketing, operations, and ethics. The second year offered specializations and electives, allowing students to explore areas like finance, strategy, and development management. Over time, both institutions expanded to include doctoral programs, executive education, and consulting divisions.

Faculty were encouraged to conduct applied research, collaborate with government agencies, and engage with civil society—further reinforcing the idea that management was a discipline with societal relevance.

The Legacy Begins

By the end of the 1970s, both IIM Ahmedabad and IIM Calcutta had:

- ✓ Created a national brand for management education

- ✓ Contributed alumni who would go on to lead India's most respected corporations, civil services, and entrepreneurial ventures

- ✓ Developed a reputation for rigor, excellence, and social contribution

- ✓ Inspired the creation of more IIMs and business schools across the country

Their success demonstrated that India could not only import educational models—but also adapt, evolve, and lead.

By the late 1970s, both IIM Ahmedabad and IIM Calcutta had moved from experimental status to national icons. Their alumni were beginning to populate the highest levels of Indian industry, bureaucracy, and policy-making. Graduates became CEOs, government advisors, NGO founders, and educators. They carried with them the ethos of their alma maters—rigor, relevance, and responsibility. The institutions, too, had matured—building permanent campuses, attracting international faculty, publishing research, and influencing public discourse on economic and administrative issues.

Perhaps the most enduring legacy of these institutions was that they fundamentally changed how leadership was imagined in India. The IIMs did not just train managers; they created a new archetype—the professional Indian manager, equipped with both analytical tools and ethical grounding, capable of navigating the complexity of a fast-evolving nation. These were not just job seekers; they were problem-solvers, innovators, and institution-builders. Their influence extended far beyond corporate boardrooms—they entered public sector undertakings, state planning boards, international agencies, and entrepreneurial ventures that would help define India's economic destiny.

Looking back, it becomes clear that the story of IIM Ahmedabad and IIM Calcutta is not just a chapter in the history of education—it is a chapter in the making of modern India. It is a story of how global collaboration, when guided by local wisdom, can create institutions that are globally benchmarked yet deeply rooted. It is a story of how bold visions, when matched with action, can redefine a nation's future.

In the chapters ahead, we will see how these two institutes inspired a movement—a proliferation of IIMs and business schools across India, each seeking to replicate the success of IIMA and IIMC, while evolving in their own unique contexts. But the foundation was laid here, in the shared classrooms, chalkboards, and case discussions of Ahmedabad and Calcutta. The rest, as they say, is legacy.

IIM Calcutta: The MIT Sloan Connection

Founded in November 1961, IIM Calcutta was the first IIM to become operational, Its academic partnership with MIT Sloan School of Management shaped its early curriculum and philosophy.

Key Highlights:

- Emphasis on quantitative techniques, systems analysis, and operations research

- Structured programs in decision science, econometrics, and management theory

- Early adoption of computers and data analysis, reflecting MIT's technological focus

- Faculty development through MIT-led training, co-teaching, and curriculum sharing

The collaboration gave IIM Calcutta a technocratic identity, producing graduates who were analytical, research-oriented, and aligned with the industrialization goals of India's Five-Year Plans.

IIM Ahmedabad: The Harvard Blueprint

Launched shortly after IIMC, IIM Ahmedabad quickly emerged as a model of contextualized excellence. With strong backing from Dr. Vikram Sarabhai, it partnered with Harvard Business School, known globally for its case method pedagogy.

Key Features of the Collaboration:

- Introduction of the cese-based learning model, focusing on real-world business problems
- A faculty-led governance structure promoting academic autonomy and innovation
- Co-creation of courses tailored to Indian business and administrative contexts
- Exposure to global business ethics, leadership development, and participatory pedagogy

Harvard faculty visited Ahmedabad regularly, while Indian professors were trained at HBS. This exchange embedded a culture of academic excellence, critical thinking, and classroom interaction.

CHAPTER EIGHT

The Spread and Standardization

How IIMs Became a National Movement and Management Education Found Its Model: The early success of IIM Calcutta and IIM Ahmedabad in the 1960s had proven that India could create world-class institutions in management education—institutions that were rooted in Indian needs but benchmarked against global standards. However, the challenge before the nation was far greater than what two elite schools could address. By the 1970s and 1980s, India's economy was expanding across multiple dimensions. Public sector undertakings (PSUs) were booming, new industries like information technology and telecommunications were emerging, and infrastructure development was demanding capable project management. From central ministries to cooperative societies, from state governments to growing private enterprises, the need for skilled managers became not just a corporate requirement but a national imperative.

It was in this context that the Indian Institutes of Management began their transformation from standalone pioneers to a nationally coordinated movement. The idea of one or two IIMs serving a country of over 600 districts and 1 billion people was simply untenable. The government, academia, and industry all recognized that the IIM model needed to be replicated across regions, both to democratize access to quality management education and to align local leadership development with national priorities. What followed was a strategic and phased expansion of the IIM network across the country. Each new institute carried the same DNA—autonomy, academic rigor, and societal purpose—while also embracing regional flavors and contextual adaptations.

The first to follow in this expansion was the Indian Institute of Management Bangalore, established in 1973. Located in India's emerging technology and public sector hub, IIM Bangalore was designed to serve the growing industries of southern India. It brought management education closer to the ecosystems of aerospace, public enterprises, and, later, the information technology revolution that would reshape the region. IIM Bangalore also emerged as a bridge between management and policy. Its early engagement with defense research institutions, public policy departments, and software companies created a unique niche that blended managerial competence with developmental foresight. Over time, IIMB also became known for its strong academic programs in entrepreneurship and innovation—tapping into Bengaluru's rise as the startup capital of India.

The next phase of expansion came with IIM Lucknow in 1984. As the first IIM in north-central India, it had a dual mission: to bring the IIM legacy to the heart of the Hindi-speaking belt and to support public administration in one of India's most complex governance landscapes. IIM Lucknow embraced this responsibility with programs focused on rural development, human resource management, and small enterprise support. It was among the first IIMs to establish a satellite campus in Noida, catering specifically to working professionals, civil servants, and executive learners. Through this outreach, IIML not only expanded the geographical reach of management education but also diversified its social base—serving aspirants from small towns, public service backgrounds, and underserved regions.

New IIMs: Expanding the Vision

IIM Bangalore (est, 1973)

- Located in India's emerging tech hub
- Emphasized corporate interface and public policy
- Played a key role in bridging academia and industry in southern India

IIM Lucknow (est. 1984)

- Focused on northern India's educationdevelopment
- Introduced rural management, entrepreneurship, and leadership programs

IIM Indore (est. 1996)

- Created to meet central India's growing business education needs
- Became a pioneer in launching the5-year IIntegrated Program in Management (IPM)

IIM Kozhikode (est. 1996)

- The first IIM in Kerala, promoting inclusive education and digital learning
- Later became a leader in online executive education

Each new IIM was designed with a core philosophy of autonomy, excellence, and relevance, yet allowed to innovate in curriculum, focus areas, and pedagogy based on regional and national needs.

The 1990s brought further transformation. India's economic liberalization, launched in 1991, unleashed a wave of private sector growth and globalization. This created unprecedented demand for MBAs and business leaders who could navigate open markets, multinational collaborations, and digital technologies. The response came in the form of two new IIMs—Indore and Kozhikode—both established in 1996. IIM Indore was created to serve central India, and it quickly distinguished itself through innovation. It became the first IIM to offer a five-year Integrated Program in Management (IPM), allowing students to enter the IIM system directly after Class 12. This was a radical departure from the traditional post-graduate MBA model and signaled IIM Indore's commitment to experimentation, youth engagement, and long-term leadership development.

Meanwhile, IIM Kozhikode extended the IIM footprint into the culturally rich and educationally advanced state of Kerala. Situated on a picturesque hilltop campus, the institute developed a reputation for academic discipline, global linkages, and digital pedagogy. It was among the first IIMs to achieve significant gender diversity in its classrooms and pioneered Interactive Distance Learning (IDL) programs that reached working professionals across India. IIM Kozhikode's emphasis on inclusivity, technological innovation, and academic integrity made it a model for new-age management education.

As these institutions grew, so did the need for standardization. The introduction of the Common Admission Test (CAT) as a unified entrance exam for all IIMs brought a level of meritocracy and transparency that was rare in India's education system. The CAT ensured that admission was based purely on aptitude and potential, rather than geography or privilege. Over time, CAT scores also became the benchmark for dozens of other top management institutions across the country, creating a standardized pipeline for aspirants from every corner of India.

The expansion of the IIM system also coincided with the rise of regulatory frameworks like the All India Council for Technical Education (AICTE), which began to oversee the explosion of non-IIM business schools in the country. While the IIMs remained largely autonomous, AICTE's guidelines helped bring minimum quality standards to thousands of private and public institutions offering MBA and PGDM programs. The 1980s and 1990s thus became a period of simultaneous expansion and standardization. Management education became scalable, structured, and nationally integrated. The term "MBA" became aspirational—no longer limited to metro cities or elite families, but increasingly accessible to students from Tier 2 and Tier 3 towns.

Even as the IIM network grew, its core principles remained intact. Each new IIM was expected to adhere to certain non-negotiables: faculty-led governance, curricular autonomy, peer-reviewed research, industry interaction, and a commitment to both private sector excellence and public sector relevance. These guiding principles allowed the IIMs to maintain their institutional credibility even as they diversified across regions, cultures, and economies.

By the late 1990s, the "IIM tag" had become a symbol of prestige, professionalism, and potential. Graduates from any of the IIMs were highly sought after—not just in India but increasingly in international job markets as well. The placement process, once a modest affair, became a full-fledged industry in itself—drawing recruiters from consulting giants, global banks, FMCG companies, and tech firms. The MBA from an IIM was now seen not only as a degree, but as a life-changing credential. It opened doors, changed family trajectories, and positioned its holders for leadership roles in every conceivable sector.

Standardization Through CAT and AICTE

As IIMs grew in number, a need arose to streamline admissions and ensure uniform standards.

The Common Admission Test (CAT) became the national gateway to IIMs and many other top B-schools. Its rigorous format ensured meritocracy and standardization across the ecosystem.

The All India Council for Technical Education (AICTE), established in 1987, began regulating hon-IIM management institutions to ensure baseline quality in curriculum, infrastructure, and faculty.

The UGC and Ministry of HRD introduced frameworks to accredit and monitor business schools, attempting to control the quality explosion that would come in the 1990s.

This era marked the birth of the MBA brand in India—prestigious, powerful, and standardized.

This era marked the birth of the MBA brand in India—prestigious, powerful, and standardized.

This success also had a multiplier effect. Inspired by the IIM model, several other institutions began to emerge, adopting similar governance structures, curricular designs, and admission processes. Schools like XLRI Jamshedpur, SP Jain Institute of Management and Research (SPJIMR), Management Development Institute (MDI) Gurgaon, and NMIMS Mumbai adopted many elements of the IIM framework—especially the emphasis on industry engagement, academic freedom, and performance-driven culture. While some of these schools had existed before the newer IIMs, the IIM standard helped elevate expectations across the entire business education ecosystem.

At the policy level, the University Grants Commission (UGC), AICTE, and the Ministry of Human Resource Development (now Ministry of Education) began to support accreditation frameworks that encouraged institutional transparency, outcome measurement, and accountability. These efforts aimed to preserve quality even as the number of management institutions ballooned—from just a handful in the 1980s to over 3,000 by the 2000s.

However, this rapid growth also brought challenges. Critics began to question whether the focus on placements had overtaken the focus on learning. The standardization, while useful for scale, sometimes led to curricular rigidity and intellectual monotony. Innovation in pedagogy, interdisciplinarity, and social orientation often took a backseat to rankings and placement salaries. Moreover, faculty shortages, limited research output, and uneven quality plagued many second- and third-tier schools.

And yet, the IIMs continued to set the benchmark. Their success was not just academic—it was philosophical. They proved that high-quality management education could be built in India, for India, and eventually for the world. They demonstrated that institutions rooted in autonomy, mission-driven leadership, and academic excellence could thrive despite limited resources and complex governance environments.

Defining the Indian MBA Model

While influenced by American and European systems, Indian management education developed its own identity:

- ☑ Heavy reliance on entrance exams and academic rigor

- ☑ Mix of case-based and lecture-based pedagogy

- ☑ Inclusion of socio-economic development, not just profit-making

- ☑ Emphasis on placement outcomes as a measure of success

- ☑ Growing focus on entrepreneurship, ethics, and innovation

This standardized approach helped management education become scalable and accessible, but also brought challenges—especially around curriculum rigidity, academic diversity, and practical relevance.

In conclusion, the spread and standardization of IIMs and their influence on Indian management education created not just a network of elite schools but a scalable national model. This model combined global ideas with local execution, professional ambition with societal purpose. It produced a generation of leaders who could navigate boardrooms and grassroots projects with equal ease. As India entered the 21st century—ready to embrace globalization, digitalization, and demographic transformation—it was this institutional infrastructure, laid over decades, that would serve as its intellectual backbone.

The next chapters of the B-School saga will show how these institutions adapted to liberalization, engaged with technology, and responded to new-age challenges. But the foundation—the IIM blueprint, its values, and its governance—remains one of the greatest achievements in the history of Indian higher education.

Part III: The Private B-School Boom

CHAPTER NINE

Liberalization and the Rise of Private B-Schools

How India's Economic Reforms Created a New Era of Business Education: In 1991, India stood at an inflection point. A balance of payments crisis forced the country to initiate a wave of economic reforms that would change its course forever. The liberalization, privatization, and globalization (LPG) policies initiated under Prime Minister P.V. Narasimha Rao and Finance Minister Dr. Manmohan Singh didn't merely restructure the economy—they redefined the aspirations of a nation. In the years that followed, a new India emerged: one that was market-driven, entrepreneurial, and globally engaged. And at the heart of this transformation was a new demand—for leaders, for thinkers, for professional managers who could steer the country through its newfound economic complexities. The public institutions that had pioneered management education, like the IIMs, were no longer sufficient to cater to this explosive demand. A new era had begun—ushered in by a wave of private business schools that would democratize access to management education and reimagine its delivery.

The effects of liberalization were far-reaching. As restrictions lifted and industries opened up, sectors like IT, telecom, banking, insurance, retail, and consumer goods began to grow at unprecedented rates. Foreign direct investment (FDI) poured in. Indian companies went global. Startups became aspirational. And with this economic dynamism came an urgent need for professionals who could manage scale, competition, and cross-border operations. The MBA, once a niche and elite credential, became the degree of choice for a rising middle class hungry for social mobility and financial security. Parents saw it as a smart investment. Students saw it as a launchpad to upward mobility. And the private sector saw an opportunity.

Private B-schools began mushrooming across India—first in metropolitan hubs like Mumbai, Delhi, and Bangalore, and soon after in Tier 2 and Tier 3 cities like Pune, Indore, Bhubaneswar, and Coimbatore. These schools catered to a wider demographic, bringing management education closer to students who had neither the networks nor the access to reach an IIM. Many were founded by education entrepreneurs, philanthropists, or corporate groups who believed that the future of India lay in producing skilled business professionals. They offered promises of placements, industry exposure, personality development, and soft skills—all packaged in slick brochures and urban campuses.

Some institutions stood out as pioneers, setting new benchmarks for private B-schools in India. The Indian School of Business (ISB), launched in Hyderabad in 2001, was a game-changer. Founded by corporate leaders and supported by the likes of McKinsey, ISB introduced India's first globally benchmarked one-year MBA program. It wasn't just the format that was new—it was the vision.

ISB partnered with Wharton, Kellogg, and London Business School to bring global faculty and pedagogy to Indian soil. It targeted mid-career professionals, offering them a fast-tracked, high-impact learning experience that rivaled the best international programs. In doing so, ISB disrupted the traditional two-year MBA model and proved that India could not only consume but also create world-class management education.

The Emergence of Private B-Schools

With limited seats in IIMs and other government institutions, the private sector responded swiftly:

- Hundreds of private business schools were established across metropolitan and Tier 2/3 cities

- These schools promised corporate exposure, soft skills training, industry-aligned curricula, and most importantly, campus placements

- Some were backed by corporate groups, others by philanthropists, and many by education entrepreneurs

This era saw the emergence of now-renowned institutions like:

Indian School of Business (ISB), Hyderabad

SPJIMR, Mumbai (repositioned itself with unique pedagogical innovations)

Amity Business School, Noida

Symbiosis Institute of Business Management (SIBM), Pune

Great Lakes Institute of Management, Chennai

NMIMS, Mumbai

These institutions often differentiated themselves through niche specializations, global collaborations, executive education offerings, and hybrid learning formats.

Around the same time, other private institutions began to shine in their own ways. SPJIMR in Mumbai reinvented itself by embedding Indian ethos into modern business thinking. It introduced innovative modules like Development of Corporate Citizenship (DOCC), where students worked with NGOs across India. XLRI Jamshedpur, although established in 1949, rose to national prominence during this period for its strong HRM program and ethical leadership model rooted in Jesuit values. MDI Gurgaon capitalized on its proximity to India's corporate capital to become a favorite among recruiters and executive learners. NMIMS Mumbai transformed from a commerce college into a multi-disciplinary university, while Symbiosis in Pune created an entire ecosystem of professional institutes catering to management, law, and media.

What united these institutions was their ability to respond to the market with speed, innovation, and relevance. They were agile in updating curricula, flexible in delivery formats, and proactive in industry engagement. They built strong alumni networks, hosted international faculty, and offered experiential learning through live projects, case studies, and immersion programs. Importantly, they emphasized student empowerment. Unlike the rigid structures of many public universities, these schools promoted student-led clubs, peer learning platforms, and entrepreneurial incubation—giving students a sense of ownership in their education.

However, the rapid growth of private B-schools was not without its pitfalls. As demand soared, so did supply—often unchecked. At one point, India had over 3,000 institutions offering MBA or PGDM programs, many of them subpar in quality and driven more by commercial motives than academic vision. While top-tier private schools flourished, a long tail of institutions struggled with inadequate faculty, poor infrastructure, and weak industry linkages. The result was an oversupply of MBA graduates with limited employability, leading to growing skepticism about the true value of the degree.

Regulators like the All India Council for Technical Education (AICTE) attempted to step in by setting minimum norms and standards. They introduced frameworks for faculty-student ratios, campus infrastructure, curriculum guidelines, and admissions protocols. But enforcement remained inconsistent, and many institutions continued to operate in gray zones. Some offered degrees without accreditation, others overpromised on placements, and a few were little more than degree shops. For every SPJIMR or ISB, there were dozens of schools that fell short of basic academic expectations.

And yet, despite this uneven landscape, the contribution of private B-schools to India's management education ecosystem is undeniable. They made the MBA accessible to a much broader base. They expanded diversity—not just in gender, but in academic background, geography, and socio-economic status. They compelled traditional institutions to evolve, to modernize their curriculum, invest in infrastructure, and engage more deeply with industry. They also played a crucial role in building India's talent pool during the IT and services boom, supplying project managers, analysts, consultants, and team leads to both Indian and multinational companies.

Several niche institutions also emerged during this period, filling specific gaps in the managerial talent landscape. MICA in Ahmedabad became a premier destination for marketing and communication. IRMA in Anand focused on rural management and cooperative enterprises. NIBM in Pune catered to banking professionals, while NIFM in Faridabad specialized in public finance. These schools served sectors that were often overlooked by mainstream MBA programs, creating domain-specific experts who could operate in specialized roles with both depth and dexterity.

As the 2000s progressed, private B-schools began to invest heavily in global engagement. Many sought international accreditations like AACSB, EQUIS, and AMBA. Exchange programs, dual-degree collaborations, and faculty mobility with universities abroad became common. The classroom became more cosmopolitan. Case studies included global companies. Students graduated not just with Indian knowledge but with global confidence. The MBA was no longer just a professional qualification—it became a personal transformation journey.

The liberalization era had thus done something extraordinary—it turned business education from a bureaucratic domain into an aspirational movement. It empowered students to think of themselves not just as job seekers but as value creators, intrapreneurs, and changemakers. It gave rise to an entire sector of educational entrepreneurship. And it showed that institutions built with vision, agility, and integrity could thrive even without state support.

But with expansion came saturation. By the end of the 2010s, the sheen had begun to wear off. The mismatch between MBA supply and corporate demand had created an employability crisis. Critics pointed to bloated curricula, outdated teaching methods, and overemphasis on placements. EdTech startups began offering alternatives to traditional MBAs through online, modular, and skills-based programs. Industry started questioning whether B-schools were producing thinkers or just test-takers. And the once-glorified MBA faced an identity question: What is the real purpose of management education in a world that is fast-changing, digital, and uncertain?

These were questions that would come to dominate the next phase of the B-school saga. The challenge was no longer about access—it was about relevance. No longer about expansion—but about innovation. And no longer about imitation—but about creating an Indian model of management education that blended wisdom with impact.

The Promise and Perils of the Boom

While the rise of private B-schools democratized access and expanded opportunities, it also brought challenges:

Many institutions focused heavily on infrastructure and placements, but compromised on faculty quality, research, and academic rigor

The AICTE struggled to regulate the sheer number of mushrooming institutes—some of which were substandard or purely commercial

The MBA became commoditized, with over 3,000 institutions at one point offering PGDM/MBA programs of widely varying quality

Mismatch between curriculum and industry needs led to growing concerns about employability

The result was a dual reality: a few high-quality private B-schools flourished, while many others struggled to sustain relevance or student trust.

The rise of private B-schools, in all its complexities, remains one of the most significant outcomes of India's economic reforms. It symbolized ambition, resilience, and adaptability. It brought management education to the masses. It produced professionals who powered India's rise on the global economic stage. And it reminded us that education, when aligned with purpose and freedom, can transform not just careers—but nations.

CHAPTER TEN

The Emergence of ISB

Reimagining Business Education for a Global India: By the dawn of the 21st century, India stood at the cusp of a new identity—global in ambition, confident in capability, and eager to redefine its economic destiny. Liberalization had done its work; a new generation of businesses was rising, led by professionals rather than proprietors, shaped by competition rather than protectionism. The Indian economy, once hesitant and bureaucratic, was transforming into a bold marketplace of ideas, industries, and opportunities. In this fast-changing landscape, there was a growing realization that management education too needed to evolve—not incrementally, but fundamentally.Enter the Indian School of Business (ISB), Hyderabad. Founded in 2001, ISB was not an extension of the existing IIM framework—it was a fresh start, built on a global template, tailored for a new India. In vision, structure, and delivery, ISB represented a radical departure from tradition. It was born of the belief that India didn't just need more managers—it needed a new kind of manager: globally aware, strategically agile, and capable of leading in both New York and Nagpur.

The Visionaries Behind the Institution: The conception of ISB was nothing short of audacious. Led by Rajat Gupta, then Managing Director of McKinsey & Company, and supported by other business luminaries like Anil Kumar, the idea was to build an institution that would rival the world's best—not decades later, but from the very beginning. Unlike IIMs, which were government-established and heavily subsidized, ISB was envisioned as a private, autonomous institution, deeply tied to the corporate world and infused with global academic standards.

The founding team knew they couldn't achieve this alone. They sought partnerships with global institutions that had already defined excellence in business education. Thus began ISB's collaboration with the Wharton School, Kellogg School of Management, and London Business School—three titans of global academia. These partnerships brought more than prestige; they brought pedagogy, faculty, and credibility. They helped design ISB's curriculum, shared faculty members, and guided the institute in establishing international best practices in teaching, research, and academic governance.

The One-Year PGP: A Revolutionary Format: At the heart of ISB's academic innovation was its one-year Post Graduate Program (PGP) in Management—a stark contrast to the two-year MBA format that dominated India. The target audience wasn't fresh graduates. It was professionals with at least a few years of work experience—consultants, engineers, bankers, marketers, government officers, and entrepreneurs—people who had been in the field, seen the gaps, and now wanted to level up.

This decision was revolutionary. It aligned ISB with elite global schools like INSEAD, IMD, and Kellogg, whose accelerated formats had proven successful for high-potential professionals worldwide. The one-year structure offered immense value: less opportunity cost, faster ROI, and a highly immersive, focused learning experience. ISB's PGP wasn't lighter because it was shorter—it was sharper, packing rigorous coursework into four terms: pre-term, core-term, elective-term, and capstone.

The Genesis of ISB: Vision Meets Execution

ISB was conceived by a group of Indian business leaders and professionals, including Rajat Gupta (then Managing Director of McKinsey & Co.) and Anil Kumar. They envisioned a business school that would:

- ☑ Attract mid-career professionals, not just fresh graduates
- ☑ Offer a globally benchmarked, one-year MBA program
- ☑ Be run by industry, for industry, with deep corporate involvement
- ☑ Focus on world-class faculty, research, and executive education
- ☑ Create a model that matched the best in the West, but served the needs of India and Asia

It was a bold move—India had never seen a private, independent institution attempt to compete with the IIMs on such a scale.

It was a bold move—India had never seen a private, independent institution attempt to compete with the IIMs on such a scale.

The Global Academic Partnerships

What set ISB apart from inception was its collaboration with three of the world's top business schools:

Wharton School
(University of Pennsylvania)

Kellogg School of Management
(Northwestern University)

London Business School
(UK)

These partnerships ensured:

- Access to visiting international faculty and global case studies
- Academic credibility from day one
- Best-in-class curriculum design and classroom practices
- International placements and corporate linkages

Students could choose from over 200 electives, allowing deep dives into domains like strategy, analytics, entrepreneurship, marketing, operations, and finance. The structure supported cross-functional learning and specialization, while the teaching emphasized leadership, ethics, and innovation. Within a year, ISB transformed mid-career professionals into boardroom-ready leaders—without detouring through extended academic hiatuses.

A Global Faculty Model: Perhaps ISB's most audacious academic innovation was its faculty model. Instead of building an exclusively full-time, in-house teaching team, ISB leveraged visiting faculty from partner institutions across the globe. Professors from Wharton, Kellogg, LBS, MIT Sloan, and Darden regularly taught at ISB, bringing the latest global frameworks, research, and business insights to Hyderabad.

Simultaneously, ISB recruited Indian-origin PhDs from top global institutions—professionals who had the academic training and global perspective to anchor ISB's long-term faculty needs. This dual approach—blending world-renowned visiting faculty with a growing base of research-driven permanent faculty—allowed ISB to maintain academic excellence while building its own intellectual capital over time.

The classroom at ISB became a truly global arena—one where Harvard cases met Indian market realities, where cross-border leadership was not theory but experience. Students were mentored by faculty who advised Fortune 500 firms, led policy consultations, or served on innovation boards—making ISB's academic environment intellectually stimulating and practically grounded.

Corporate-Backed, Industry-Aligned: Unlike most Indian B-schools that developed industry connections gradually through alumni networks, ISB was born with industry embedded in its DNA. Its founding board featured India's most respected business leaders—Ratan Tata, Adi Godrej, Deepak Parekh, Kumaramangalam Birla, Narayana Murthy, and others. Their presence wasn't ceremonial—it was strategic. They helped shape the school's vision, mentored batches, contributed to curriculum discussions, and provided funding for infrastructure and scholarships.

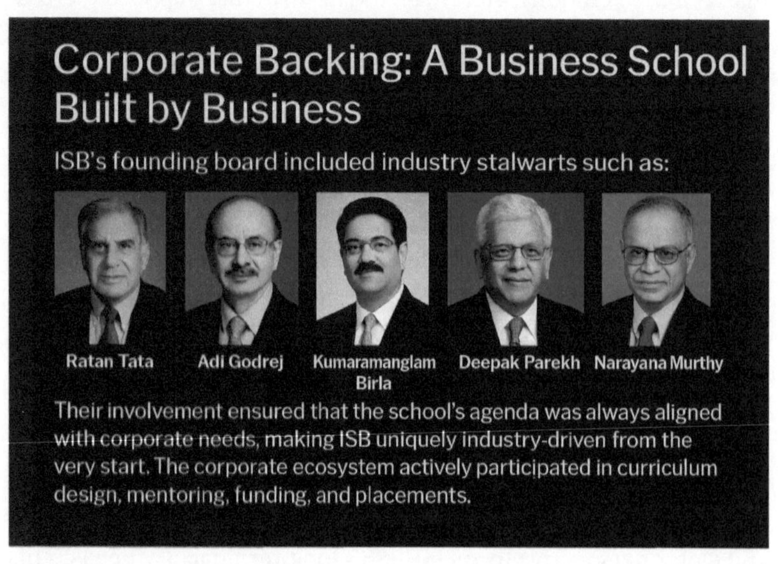

This industry connect was further institutionalized through career advancement services. ISB's placement strategy was designed not around mass hiring for entry-level roles, but around lateral placements, suited for experienced professionals. Companies like McKinsey, BCG, Amazon, Microsoft, Citibank, Unilever, and Google quickly saw the value in ISB's talent pool. ISB didn't just place graduates—it cultivated relationships that converted into advisory boards, case collaborations, guest lectures, and live projects.

In less than a decade, ISB had built what most institutions take generations to achieve—a deep, organic, and multi-layered engagement with industry.

Research and Centers of Excellence: What set ISB apart even further was its early commitment to research. It wasn't enough to teach business; ISB wanted to shape how business was thought about. To that end, it established specialized research centers such as:

- Centre for Analytical Finance
- Bharti Institute of Public Policy
- Munjal Institute for Global Manufacturing
- Max Institute of Healthcare Management
- ISB Insight (research dissemination platform)

These centers tackled real-world issues—from SME financing and healthcare innovation to regulatory reform and sustainability. They bridged the academic-industry-policy divide and gave ISB faculty the opportunity to influence public discourse, publish in top journals, and advise government and corporate stakeholders.

This research focus added an intellectual dimension to ISB's identity, positioning it not just as a teaching school, but as a knowledge institution.

Infrastructure and Branding: ISB's physical campus in Hyderabad matched its global ambitions. Spanning over 260 acres, it was designed for immersion—housing, learning, recreation, and collaboration under one roof. Smart classrooms, executive residences, international-standard auditoriums, and technology-enabled learning labs were part of its everyday fabric.

Its branding too was deliberate and consistent. ISB positioned itself as India's "Indian Ivy League"—not replicating the IIMs, but offering a globally equivalent, privately funded alternative. Its brochures, website, alumni success stories, and media presence exuded sophistication, clarity, and aspiration.

In 2012, ISB expanded its footprint by opening a second campus in Mohali, Punjab, further reinforcing its pan-India ambition. The Mohali campus housed specialized centers, including those focused on public policy and entrepreneurship, and created more regional opportunities for executive and research engagement.

Outcomes and Impact

In just two decades, ISB achieved what many considered improbable:

- It broke into the Financial Times Global MBA Rankings, becoming the youngest B-school to do so.
- It placed thousands of graduates in top global firms, government positions, startups, and social enterprises.
- Its alumni network, now over 16,000 strong, includes unicorn founders, corporate CXOs, bureaucrats, and change-makers.
- It inspired other Indian institutions—including IIMs—to launch one-year executive and MBA programs.

It redefined Indian management education by showing that quality need not be publicly subsidized, and excellence could be entrepreneurial.

Criticisms and Challenges

- Like all institutions that break new ground, ISB hasn't been free from critique:
- Its high tuition fees have raised questions of affordability and elitism.
- Its initial over-reliance on visiting faculty invited concerns about continuity and cultural alignment.
- The absence of an undergraduate pipeline limited its ability to shape early talent.
- Its global placements, while strong, are still evolving in scale compared to top-tier Western schools.

Yet, ISB has consistently addressed these challenges through innovation, outreach, and academic investment. Its alumni network, brand equity, and employer trust have only grown stronger with time.

A Private Pioneer with a Public Mission: The Indian School of Business didn't emerge from legacy—it emerged from vision. It didn't follow the path set by others—it created its own. It didn't ask for public support—it built excellence through private initiative, global collaboration, and relentless execution.

More than a B-school, ISB became a statement: that India, at the turn of the millennium, was ready to lead—not just in software or services, but in shaping the minds that would run the world's most complex organizations.

ISB's model redefined what a business school could be—fast, flexible, globally connected, and deeply industry-oriented. In doing so, it didn't compete with the IIMs—it complemented them, offering a parallel track for experienced professionals who wanted more than a degree: they wanted transformation.

In the next chapter, we will explore how this rapid expansion—of IIMs and private institutions alike—led to new challenges of regulation, quality assurance, and the evolving role of AICTE, UGC, and accreditation bodies in safeguarding the future of business education in India.

CHAPTER ELEVEN

AICTE, Accreditation, and Regulation:

Bringing Order to India's Management Education Ecosystem: As India entered the new millennium, the map of management education began to mirror the broader economy—vibrant, fragmented, and rapidly expanding. The liberalization reforms of the early 1990s had unlocked vast opportunities in sectors like IT, finance, telecom, and retail, creating a hunger for managerial talent. This hunger, in turn, gave rise to an explosion of business schools across the country—private and public, urban and rural, elite and aspiring. But with expansion came disorder. As the number of institutions multiplied, questions of credibility, consistency, and quality became impossible to ignore.

India, once home to a handful of elite management institutions like the IIMs, suddenly had over 3,000 business schools. The surge brought diversity in models, but also confusion and concern. Could all these institutions deliver the same value? Did the term "MBA" mean the same across campuses? Were students being equipped for success, or were they being sold a dream without substance? These questions pointed to a clear need: regulation, standardization, and quality assurance.

It was in this context that regulatory bodies like the AICTE (All India Council for Technical Education), UGC (University Grants Commission), and accreditation agencies like NBA (National Board of Accreditation) and NAAC (National Assessment and

Accreditation Council) began to play an increasingly central role in shaping India's management education ecosystem.

AICTE: The Apex Regulator of Technical and Management Education

Though originally established in 1945 as an advisory body, AICTE was granted statutory authority in 1987 to oversee technical education across India. Over time, its role expanded to include management education—particularly the regulation of standalone institutions offering Post Graduate Diploma in Management (PGDM) programs.

AICTE's mandate was both simple and significant: ensure that institutions offering management education adhered to minimum standards of quality. It approved new programs, fixed intake capacities, evaluated infrastructure, faculty qualifications, and pedagogy. Periodic inspections and audits were introduced to ensure compliance. In cases of violation, AICTE had the authority to suspend approvals or recommend closure.

In a market filled with private players—some excellent, others dubious—AICTE acted as the gatekeeper. Its approval became a prerequisite for legitimacy, particularly for PGDM programs, which, unlike university-affiliated MBAs, didn't carry degree status under UGC norms.

But AICTE's role was not just restrictive. Over the years, it introduced model curricula, pushed for internships, encouraged faculty development programs, and emphasized outcome-based education. In doing so, it attempted to transition from being a watchdog to a facilitator of quality improvement.

Key Roles of AICTE in B-School Regulation

☑ Granting approval for opening or expanding MBA/PGDM programs

☑ Ensuring minimum standards for faculty, Infrastructure, and curriculum

☑ Conducting periodic inspections and reviews

☑ Approving seat intake and monitoring admissions processes

☑ Recommending closure of non-compliant institutions

AICTE's intent was to bring uniformity, transparency, and accountability—especially in a space that had begun to suffer from over-commercialization.

UGC: The University Anchor

While AICTE regulated autonomous institutions, the University Grants Commission (UGC) governed the vast universe of university-affiliated MBA programs. These programs, offered by central, state, private, and deemed universities, followed UGC guidelines on syllabi, examination structures, degree issuance, and academic frameworks.

Unlike PGDM programs, these MBAs were full-fledged degrees and often came with greater public trust due to the university tag. However, UGC's focus was more on academic legitimacy than on market relevance. This occasionally led to criticism that many university MBA programs remained outdated, overly theoretical, and disconnected from the demands of the modern economy.

The dual regulatory structure—AICTE for PGDM and UGC for MBA—created confusion for students. Many struggled to understand whether a PGDM was "inferior" to an MBA or vice versa. In reality, some PGDM institutions outperformed MBAs in curriculum quality and industry interface. But the lack of a unified framework often blurred these distinctions, leaving aspirants dependent on brand perception rather than regulatory clarity.

Accreditation: Beyond Approval, Towards Assurance

As the number of B-schools grew, a more nuanced form of quality assessment became essential. This led to the rise of accreditation agencies like NBA and NAAC, which moved beyond regulatory approval to assess educational quality on measurable outcomes.

The National Board of Accreditation (NBA), initially part of AICTE but later made autonomous, focused on program-level accreditation. Unlike AICTE's input-based approval (infrastructure, faculty ratio, etc.), NBA emphasized outcome-based education (OBE). It asked critical questions: Were students learning what they were supposed to? Were they employable? Was the institution producing value?

The NBA's rigorous peer-review process evaluated pedagogy, research output, industry collaboration, student progression, and governance. Accredited programs gained recognition not just in India but under the Washington Accord, enhancing global acceptability.

On the other hand, NAAC assessed institutional quality—including governance, innovation, teaching processes, and social responsibility. It rated universities and colleges on a cumulative grade point average, with "A+" and "A" ratings becoming badges of pride.

Over time, accreditation became a differentiator in a crowded marketplace. Students used it as a marker of trust, while institutions used it to attract faculty, funding, and partnerships.

The Global Push: AACSB, AMBA, EQUIS

Indian B-Schools Aligning with Global Benchmarks
As Indian business schools set their sights on global recognition, many turned to prestigious international accreditations to validate their quality and enhance their global standing.

- AACSB (Association to Advance Collegiate Schools of Business)
- AMBA (Association of MBAs)
- EQUIS (EFMD Quality Improvement System)

Top institutions like ISB, IIM Calcutta, IIM Bangalore, and SPJIMR successfully secured these international badges of excellence—joining a select group of globally benchmarked B-schools.

The Global Push:
AACSB, AMBA, EQUIS

As Indian B-schools aspired to global standards, many sought international accreditations:

AACSB (Association to Advance Collegiate Schools of Business)

AMBA (Association of MBAs)

EQUIS (EFMD Quality Improvement System)

Institutions like ISB, IIM Calcutta, IIM Bangalore, and SPJIMR earned these stamps of excellence, placing them alongside the world's best.-These accreditations evaluated everything–mission clarity, faculty quality, research output, alumni success, and employer reputatiòn.

For globally-minded students and recruiters, such accreditations became a signal that an Indian B-school could match Harvard, INSEAD, or LBS– not just in ambition, but in execution.

These accreditations assess schools on a wide range of criteria: clarity of mission, faculty credentials, research excellence, student outcomes, alumni impact, and employer perception.

Achieving them signals a school's commitment to continuous improvement, global relevance, and academic integrity.

For globally-minded students and recruiters, such accreditations became a signal that an Indian B-school could match Harvard, INSEAD, or LBS—not just in ambition, but in execution.

Rankings and Ratings: Market-Driven Quality Signals

In parallel with regulatory frameworks, the market created its own validation systems. Rankings by media houses (India Today, Outlook, Business Today, The Economic Times) became annual rituals. Parameters included faculty-student ratio, salary packages, alumni strength, industry interface, and perception scores.

Later, the National Institutional Ranking Framework (NIRF) introduced by the Ministry of Education brought more objectivity—using data on teaching, research, perception, and outreach. Yet, rankings remained contentious. Institutions often gamed metrics, and the weightage given to marketing and infrastructure drew criticism. Still, in the absence of universal standards, rankings became the go-to guide for students navigating a maze of B-schools.

The Quality vs. Quantity Dilemma: India's biggest paradox in management education was this: while the number of institutions skyrocketed, quality did not always follow. Reports showed that only a small fraction of MBA graduates—7 to 10% by some estimates—were employable in top-tier roles. The rest faced low-paying jobs, weak industry exposure, and a poor return on investment.

This reality led to a proliferation of degree-holding, job-seeking graduates, many of whom felt betrayed by the promise of a better life through an MBA. It raised fundamental questions: Was regulation failing? Were accreditations symbolic? Could massification coexist with mastery?

The problem was not access. It was quality. B-schools mushroomed without adequate faculty, without updated curriculum, without digital readiness or entrepreneurial orientation. Regulatory bodies often struggled to shut down poor performers, while political interference, resource constraints, and bureaucratic delays made enforcement patchy.

Enter NEP 2020: A Roadmap for Reform: In 2020, the National Education Policy (NEP) offered a glimmer of hope. It proposed a single Higher Education Commission of India (HECI) to replace the maze of UGC, AICTE, and other bodies. It envisioned:

- Institutional autonomy with accountability
- A shift from input-based to outcome-based regulation
- Interdisciplinary education and credit transfer
- Stronger focus on research, innovation, and internationalization

For management education, NEP's message was clear: empower institutions to innovate, but make them responsible for outcomes. Accreditation, curriculum design, and even fee models would be liberalized—but excellence would be non-negotiable.

The Way Forward: Regulation with Vision - The journey of regulating business education in India has always walked a tightrope—between freedom and control, expansion and quality, access and excellence. Institutions like AICTE and UGC have played critical roles in setting benchmarks, but their effectiveness has been uneven. Accreditation bodies like NBA and NAAC have pushed for deeper accountability, but adoption remains limited to better-funded institutions.

The future demands a new regulatory philosophy—one that sees institutions as partners, not suspects. It must move from control to enablement, from paper compliance to performance metrics, from bureaucracy to academic entrepreneurship.

Most importantly, it must ensure that management education in India not only produces more MBAs—but better ones. MBAs who can manage not just businesses, but impact. Who understand not just markets, but missions. Who can lead not just companies, but communities.

Creating Institutions, Not Just Institutions of Approval: India's regulatory framework for management education is evolving—from an era of approval and inspection to one of accreditation and autonomy. The new era demands not just compliance, but commitment—to outcomes, to learners, to society.

As the country moves toward becoming a Viksit Bharat by 2047, its business schools must be engines of innovation, inclusion, and leadership. Regulation will continue to play a vital role—but it must do so with vision, flexibility, and trust.

After all, the best regulation is not what controls institutions, but what enables them to rise.

Part IV: The Changing Face of Business Education

CHAPTER TWELVE

From Classrooms to Online: Tech Disruption

In a world where industries are disrupted overnight and knowledge becomes obsolete in months, the business of educating future managers is under constant pressure to evolve. Over the last two decades, Indian management education has undergone a digital transformation that has radically changed the way MBAs are taught, learned, and experienced. The classroom, once defined by chalkboards, lecture notes, and rigid timetables, has now become a dynamic, fluid, and often virtual space where technology mediates every interaction. Indian business schools have been at the frontlines of this shift—sometimes as reluctant adopters, and at other times as bold pioneers. This chapter traces the unfolding of this disruption, with a special focus on the COVID-19 pandemic, the rise of EdTech, the advent of hybrid MBAs, and the shifting identity of the Indian MBA.

The seeds of this digital revolution were sown well before the global health crisis of 2020. By the late 2000s and early 2010s, institutions such as ISB, IIM Bangalore, and Great Lakes were already experimenting with Learning Management Systems (LMS), digital case repositories, and virtual simulation tools. Platforms like Moodle, Blackboard, and Canvas became integral to managing coursework, tracking progress, and delivering content asynchronously. Faculty members started recording lectures, curating digital reading materials, and hosting virtual case competitions. Online certifications from Coursera, edX, and Udemy began finding their way into student resumes and even formal curricula. These incremental steps created a digital undercurrent that would later form the foundation of a much larger transformation.

That transformation arrived with sudden force in 2020. The COVID-19 pandemic disrupted higher education like no previous event. Overnight, physical campuses became inaccessible, and faculty and students were forced to migrate to online platforms with little time to prepare. Virtual classrooms on Zoom, Microsoft Teams, and Google Meet became the new normal. Lectures were recorded, attendance was tracked digitally, and exams moved to remote proctoring tools. For institutions rooted in traditional pedagogy, this shift was jarring. Yet, within months, most B-schools had adapted. They discovered surprising advantages: geographic flexibility, greater access to international speakers, and lower costs for some operational functions. What began as a survival mechanism quickly turned into an opportunity for reinvention.

Parallel to this institutional response, a new wave of private EdTech companies emerged with offerings that directly competed with traditional MBAs. Platforms such as UpGrad, Eruditus, Simplilearn, and Talentedge began collaborating with top Indian and global universities to offer online executive education and MBA-equivalent programs. These programs, often shorter and more affordable than full-time MBAs, targeted working professionals seeking career acceleration without taking a sabbatical. Their industry-aligned content, flexibility, and placement support made them increasingly attractive. The proposition was simple yet powerful: why spend two years and Rs. 20 lakhs when you can upskill in six months from your living room and secure a promotion or a new job?

COVID-19: The Great Digital Reset

The real disruption came in 202, when the global pandemic shuttered campuses overnight. Indian B-schools were forced to move their entire teaching apparatus online within weeks. This sudden shift led to:

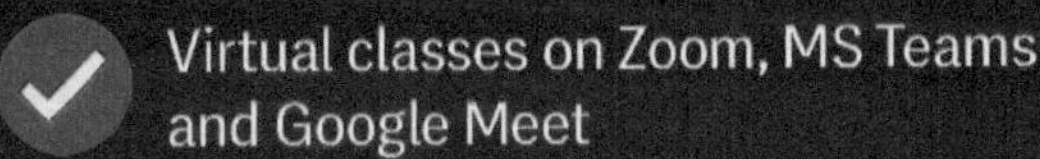 Virtual classes on Zoom, MS Teams, and Google Meet

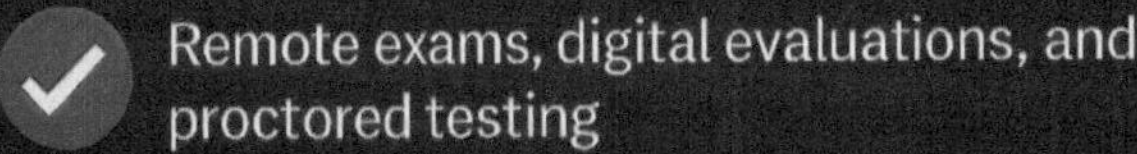 Remote exams, digital evaluations, and proctored testing

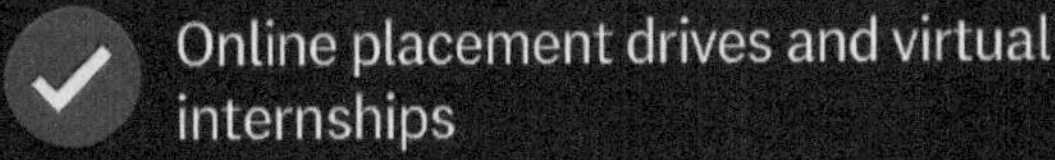 Online placement drives and virtual internships

 Increased reliance on asynchronous learning content

While the transition was chaotic, it also opened new possibilities:

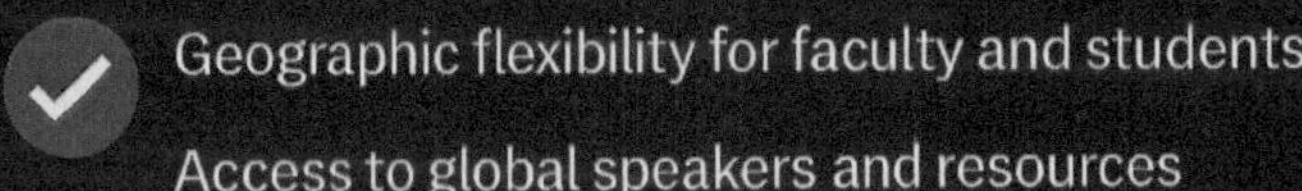 Geographic flexibility for faculty and students

Access to global speakers and resources

 Cost-saving opportunities for working professionals and institutions

COVID-19: The Great Digital Reset

This growing popularity of digital and executive programs forced traditional B-schools to rethink their models. One of the most significant outcomes was the rise of the hybrid MBA. These programs combined online coursework with occasional on-campus residencies, allowing students to benefit from both flexibility and peer interaction. Institutions like IIM Kozhikode, XLRI, BITS Pilani, and NMIMS Global rolled out hybrid formats that featured live online sessions, self-paced modules, and short-term immersions. Others, like ISB, introduced weekend-based programs like PGPpro to cater to experienced professionals. These formats redefined what an MBA could look like—less about physical presence, more about modular learning and practical engagement.

With this shift in delivery came a transformation in the curriculum itself. Business schools began to incorporate emerging fields such as artificial intelligence, data analytics, blockchain, fintech, and digital marketing into their core offerings. The learning experience became more interactive, leveraging simulations, gamified modules, and peer-reviewed projects. Capstone assignments often involved solving real-world problems for startups, NGOs, or corporations. Even soft skills training was digitized, using virtual role plays, team-building apps, and AI-driven feedback tools. The MBA classroom was no longer confined to four walls—it had become an ecosystem.

The rise of MOOCs (Massive Open Online Courses) further accelerated this transformation. Platforms like Coursera, edX, and FutureLearn brought Ivy League content to Indian students at scale, while India's own SWAYAM and NPTEL provided localized, high-quality online learning. These courses democratized access to elite business education, enabling learners from Tier 2 and Tier 3 cities to learn strategic thinking, financial modeling, and leadership from the best professors around the world. The once-clear boundary between formal and informal education began to blur, and learners started building personalized education journeys from multiple sources.

However, this digital turn was not without challenges. The digital divide became painfully evident during the pandemic. Students from economically weaker backgrounds and remote locations struggled with poor internet connectivity, lack of devices, and unsuitable home environments. Online learning also led to engagement fatigue, with students reporting reduced motivation and emotional disconnect. The traditional MBA experience—with its rich peer interactions, extracurriculars, and campus culture—was difficult to replicate online. Moreover, the explosion of certifications and online degrees raised concerns about credential inflation and employability. Recruiters began to question the value of digital credentials in the absence of rigorous quality benchmarks.

Opportunities:

Democratization of access: Students from Tier 2 and Tier 3 cities can access top-tier education

Cost optimization for both institutions and learners

Lifelong learning ecosystems supporting professionals throughout their careers

Industry integration through data-driven skill mapping and job-linked learning

Concerns:

Digital divide: Many students lack stable internet, devices, or conducive learning environments

Engagement fatigue: Online learning often suffers from reduced attention and motivation

Credential inflation: The proliferation of certifications creates confusion over credibility

Erosion of peer learning and campus experience, long seen as hallmarks

Opportunities and Concerns

Yet, amidst these challenges, the pandemic taught Indian business schools something profound: agility. Faculty who had never used a webcam were now running webinars. Institutions that once resisted online exams adopted open-book formats and AI-proctored systems. Students learned to collaborate via Slack, Miro, and Google Docs. Recruiters conducted virtual placement drives. B-schools became innovation labs in real time, adapting to uncertainty and preparing students for a world where digital fluency is no longer optional but essential.

Looking forward, the future of Indian business education is undoubtedly phygital—a seamless blend of physical and digital. Traditional classrooms will coexist with virtual ones, and degrees will be complemented by micro-credentials. Lifelong learning will become the norm, not the exception. As AI, climate change, and global disruptions reshape the business landscape, B-schools will need to shift their focus from information delivery to skill formation, character building, and real-world problem solving. Technology will be the enabler, but the vision must be human-centric.

In conclusion, the digital disruption of Indian management education is not a temporary detour but a permanent transformation. It has democratized access, increased flexibility, and sparked pedagogical innovation. But it has also raised questions about quality, credibility, and student experience. The challenge now is not whether to embrace technology, but how to do so meaningfully. The Indian MBA of the future will be judged not just by campus placements or brand rankings, but by its ability to adapt, inspire, and prepare leaders for a world in flux. If the last few years have shown us anything, it is that disruption can be a doorway to reinvention. And for Indian B-schools, that reinvention has only just begun.

CHAPTER THIRTEEN

Curriculum Evolution and Indianization of Management

Blending Global Best Practices with Bharatiya Wisdom: For decades, Indian business schools modeled their curriculum on Western management education frameworks, drawing heavily from the practices of globally acclaimed institutions like Harvard Business School, MIT Sloan, and Wharton. This alignment was strategic: it allowed India, in its post-independence nation-building phase, to produce globally competitive managers who could navigate the rapidly changing corporate environment. These early MBAs were well-versed in the case method, trained in strategic thinking, financial analysis, marketing models, and operations management, often using examples from multinational corporations in Western economies. While this approach brought academic rigor and global prestige to Indian management education, it also created a significant disconnect. Students trained to solve problems at Procter & Gamble or General Motors found themselves underprepared when working with Indian family businesses, public sector units, or rural markets. The Indian context—with its cultural, institutional, and economic complexities—often remained invisible in classrooms, leading educators to ask: Can India build a management curriculum that is both globally benchmarked and rooted in Indian realities?

The first wave of business education in India was designed with excellence in mind, but often failed to capture relevance. The curriculum at leading institutions like IIM Ahmedabad and IIM Calcutta was dominated by Western textbooks and case studies—many of which featured companies, consumers, and challenges foreign to most Indian students. The early focus was on creating corporate-ready managers, rather than nation-builders. However, as India liberalized its economy in the 1990s and embraced globalization, a new awareness emerged. Indian business was no longer imitating the West—it was innovating on its own terms. This required a new kind of manager, one who understood global frameworks but could apply them in the Indian context. Consequently, the movement for curriculum evolution began—not as a rejection of the West, but as an inclusion of the East.

A key driver of this evolution was the growing demand for contextual relevance. Management educators and industry leaders began to push for courses that addressed India's unique socio-economic landscape. Public systems management, rural marketing, microfinance, and NGO management entered the curriculum. Indian business schools began to include case studies that focused on local companies—ranging from the success of Amul and HUL in rural distribution, to the disruptive innovation of startups like Flipkart and BYJU'S. Courses on Indian family business management, ethics, and entrepreneurship were introduced, often led by professors with real-world experience in these domains. These changes helped students appreciate that Indian business was not just a derivative of Western practices—it was an ecosystem with its own logic, constraints, and opportunities.

Incorporating Indian Ethos and Thought Leaders

Many institutions began to explore the wisdom embedded in indian scriptures, history, and thought leaders to enrich leadership and values education.

- ☑ Lessons from the Bhagavad Gita on decision-making, detachment, and leadership under pressure

- ☑ Kautilya's Arthashastra as a source of insights on statecraft, economics, and strategic thinking

- ☑ Case studies on Ratan Tata, Narayana Murthy, Kiran Mazumdar-Shaw, and Verghese Kurien

- ☑ Courses inspired by Gandhian management, Swadeshi economics, and Jain business ethics

- ☑ Understanding Chhatrapati Shivaji Maharaj's leadership, Dr. A.PJ. Abdul Kalam's vision, an Swami Vivekananda's clarity of purpose

These changes were not just symbolic—they encouraged students to see India not as a market to serve, but a society to transform.

These changes were not just symbolic—they encouraged students to see India not as a market to serve, but a society to transform.

An important milestone in this journey was the integration of Indian ethos into the teaching of leadership and ethics. Drawing from ancient Indian texts like the Bhagavad Gita, Arthashastra, and Upanishads, faculty members introduced students to the philosophical foundations of duty, righteousness, self-discipline, and servant leadership. Institutions like IIM Ahmedabad and SPJIMR began offering electives on Indian Management Thought, exploring how principles of dharma and karma could inform ethical decision-making in contemporary settings. Swami Vivekananda's messages on self-confidence and nation-building, Mahatma Gandhi's approach to non-violent management, and Chanakya's strategic brilliance found their way into classrooms, offering students an ethical compass alongside managerial tools. Far from being religious or abstract, these teachings offered timeless insights into human behavior, conflict resolution, team management, and leadership under adversity.

Notably, this wasn't merely a return to tradition. The Indianization of the curriculum was about synthesis. Business schools sought to combine global frameworks with Indian insights. For instance, courses on strategy were enriched with case studies from Indian conglomerates navigating the digital age. Marketing classes included studies of rural consumer behavior and Jugaad innovation. Organizational behavior was taught alongside concepts of collectivism and community belonging, which are deeply embedded in Indian culture. As a result, Indian MBAs became better equipped not just for boardrooms in New York or London—but also for SMEs in Pune, social enterprises in Bihar, and policy think tanks in Delhi.

Notable Initiatives in Indianization

Several Indian institutions took pioneering steps in this direction:

IIM Ahmedaabad launched Initiatives on Indian Management Thought, vernacular business literature, and development sector leadership.

IIM Kozhikode introduced courses on Responsible Management and Inclusivity.

SPJIMR Mumbai embedded values-based leadership and service learning into its core curriculum.

XLRI Jamshedpur integrated Jesult principles of ethics and justice into its pedagogy.

Newer institutions like Jindal Global Business School, Flame University, and Ashoka University began blending liberal arts and management, emphasizing Indian thought in a global framework.

Each new institutions like Jindial Global Business School, Flame University, and Ashoka University began blending liberal arts and management, emphasizing Indian thought in a global framework

Institutions like IIM Kozhikode led the way in adopting the theme "India for the World," encouraging students to study Indian business models as exportable innovations. SPJIMR embedded value-based leadership, rural internships, and experiential learning into its core pedagogy. XLRI Jamshedpur emphasized the Jesuit principles of ethics and social justice, aligning business decisions with moral responsibility. Emerging private universities like Ashoka, Flame, and Jindal blended liberal arts with business education, exposing students to history, sociology, and philosophy alongside finance and strategy. These multidisciplinary approaches brought richness and diversity to the MBA experience, fostering leaders who were not just efficient, but empathetic and ethical.

Still, the Indianization of the curriculum has faced challenges. For one, there is a shortage of high-quality Indian case studies, particularly in regional languages or from the public and informal sectors. While institutions like IIM Ahmedabad and ISB have strong case-writing cells, many others lack the faculty training and resources to produce contextual material. Secondly, the pressure of placements often forces schools to focus on hard skills and corporate grooming, rather than values-based or development-focused education. There is also the risk of tokenism—where Indian content is added superficially without deep pedagogical integration. Without a national framework or accreditation guideline on Indianization, each institution interprets the concept differently—leading to inconsistency in outcomes.

A promising development in this space has been the shift from traditional case studies to caselets—short, focused narratives that explore specific management dilemmas in the Indian context. Unlike the lengthy Harvard-style cases, which may require an hour to dissect, caselets are compact and punchy, making them suitable for short discussions and blended learning formats. Indian B-schools have begun using caselets to explore a range of topics: a pricing dilemma faced by a Mumbai-based startup; an ethical conflict in a government project; or a cultural challenge in a family-run textile business. These stories are relatable, timely, and grounded in Indian realities, helping students bridge theory and practice more effectively.

Caselets have proven particularly effective in engaging students from diverse backgrounds, including those from Tier 2 and Tier 3 cities, who may find Western contexts alienating. They also work well in executive education and hybrid programs, where learning time is limited but relevance is critical. Institutions like IIMA, ISB, and IIM Indore are increasingly investing in caselet development, often collaborating with Indian companies and NGOs to document real challenges. This shift does not diminish the value of traditional case studies—it complements them by expanding the scope of learning to include diverse, indigenous, and grassroots scenarios.

One of the most profound aspects of curriculum evolution has been the integration of self-awareness and mindfulness in business education. Courses in leadership are now as much about managing oneself as managing others. Drawing from Indian traditions of yoga, meditation, and reflective journaling, students are encouraged to explore their values, biases, and emotional responses. Business schools have introduced courses on self-leadership, often beginning with a personal growth lab or inner journey module. This aligns closely with Indian philosophical thought, which places inner mastery as a prerequisite for outer success. Through this process, the MBA becomes not just a professional qualification, but a personal transformation journey.

As India emerges as a global economic power, there is a growing recognition that its management education must reflect its civilizational depth. The goal is not to create a parallel system, but a blended one—where global frameworks are adapted to local needs, and Indian philosophies are presented with academic rigor and contemporary relevance. Institutions need to go beyond adding a course or two on Indian ethos—they must weave Indian values into the entire fabric of management education. This includes admissions, pedagogy, assessments, internships, and even campus culture. Only then can the Indian MBA truly evolve from a degree to a movement.

A Call for Balanced Global-Local Integration

Indian B-schools now face the exciting challenge of designing curricula that are globally competitive yet deeply Indian in perspective. This doesn't mean rejecting Western management theories—it means adding Indian voices, experiences, and wisdom to the mix.

The future curriculum must balance:

Global Frameworks

- ✓ Harvard Case Studies
- ✓ Western Ethics
- ✓ Global Supply Chains
- ✓ AI & Digital Transformatiion

Indian Realities

- ✓ Indian MSME & Family Business Models
- ✓ Dharma-based Leadership
- ✓ Rural Distribution & Jugaad Innovation
- ✓ Technology for Social Good

In conclusion, the evolution and Indianization of the MBA curriculum is both a response to past gaps and a vision for the future. It reflects India's growing confidence in its own intellectual traditions and its ambition to create managers who are not just successful, but also socially conscious and spiritually grounded. A Bharatiya MBA is not about turning inward—it is about looking at the world through India's eyes. It is about creating leaders who think globally, act locally, and serve ethically. In doing so, Indian business schools will not only prepare students for jobs—they will prepare them for the journey of leadership in a complex, dynamic, and deeply interconnected world.

CHAPTER FOURTEEN

Leadership, Ethics, and Purpose

Redefining Success in the Indian Business School Ecosystem: For much of the twentieth century, the central aim of business education—both globally and in India—was to produce efficient managers who could drive profit, enhance productivity, and execute corporate strategies with precision. Leadership was traditionally taught as a set of managerial competencies; ethics, if included at all, was relegated to an isolated classroom discussion or a single elective; and purpose was an abstract ideal, often overlooked in favor of more tangible metrics like salary packages and shareholder value. However, in the twenty-first century, a growing number of crises—ranging from corporate fraud and environmental degradation to mental health challenges and socio-economic inequality—have forced business schools to fundamentally rethink their mission. What does it mean to be a business leader today? What should management education really prepare students for? These questions are reshaping Indian B-schools, prompting a move from producing profit-focused professionals to nurturing purpose-driven leaders.

The shift began with a series of high-profile corporate scandals and global economic disruptions that exposed the moral blind spots of even the most prestigious business institutions. In India, the collapse of Satyam, the IL&FS crisis, and banking frauds involving influential figures revealed that technical proficiency without ethical grounding could destabilize entire economies. Globally, the Enron debacle and the 2008 financial crisis signaled a systemic failure in the values being taught—or not taught—in business schools. These wake-up calls emphasized that intelligence without integrity could be dangerous. As a result, Indian business schools started reassessing their curricula, institutional cultures, and leadership development philosophies.

The contemporary reimagining of leadership in Indian B-schools reflects a broader, more humanistic understanding of what it means to lead. While traditional management theory emphasized decision-making, delegation, and driving outcomes, today's leadership frameworks include emotional intelligence, empathy, cross-cultural sensitivity, and the ability to navigate uncertainty and crisis. Programs now emphasize collaboration over competition, purpose over power, and inclusivity over hierarchy. Institutions like IIM Bangalore, ISB, and SPJIMR have introduced leadership labs, experiential learning modules, and personalized mentoring programs to help students develop self-awareness, resilience, and authenticity in their leadership styles. These are no longer soft skills—they are core competencies for 21st-century leaders.

Ethics, too, has undergone a transformation in Indian management education. It is no longer confined to an isolated course taught at the end of the semester, but is now woven into decision-making exercises, case studies, and real-world simulations across disciplines. Business Ethics and Corporate Governance are now part of the core curriculum in most IIMs and top private B-schools. Institutions like XLRI and SPJIMR have pioneered values-based education by integrating ethics into their institutional DNA. Ethical dilemmas are explored not just in the abstract, but in the messy, complex situations business leaders actually face—data privacy in tech startups, greenwashing in FMCG, whistleblowing in finance, and exploitation in global supply chains.

Leadership Reimagined: Beyond the Corner Office

In traditional management education, leadership was often equated with:

- Decision-making authority
- Vision and goal-setting
- Delegation and people management
- Driving results at scale

While these remain important, the 21st-century leader is now expected to also:

 Inspire with empathy and emotional intelligence

 Foster diversity, inclusion, and collaboration

 Lead during crises and uncertainty

 Engage with environmental and social responsibility

 Operate with transparency and authenticity

Indian B-schools began introducing leadership labs, mentoring programs, reflective exercises, and immersive fieldwork to develop these deeper traits.

Importantly, many Indian institutions have turned to the country's philosophical traditions for guidance, incorporating teachings from the Bhagavad Gita, Jainism, Buddhism, and modern icons like Gandhi, Swami Vivekananda, and A.P.J. Abdul Kalam.

Alongside leadership and ethics, the third pillar transforming Indian management education is purpose. Increasingly, MBA students are no longer satisfied with pursuing careers that simply promise high packages. Many seek meaning, mission, and a chance to contribute to something larger than themselves. Responding to this shift, B-schools are offering programs and electives that focus on social entrepreneurship, sustainable development, and responsible business. Students now undertake rural immersion programs, consult for non-profits, and work on live projects in education, healthcare, and climate change. Institutions like SPJIMR mandate Development of Corporate Citizenship (DOCC) internships, where students spend time working in grassroots organizations. IIM Udaipur has created specializations that link digital transformation with inclusive growth. These initiatives help students connect classroom learning to societal challenges and ground their ambitions in a broader sense of responsibility.

Indian B-schools are also drawing on the country's rich civilizational heritage to frame purpose-driven leadership. In ancient Indian philosophy, leadership was seen as a moral duty, or dharma, rather than a quest for status. Kings were expected to uphold the welfare of the people, guided by principles of justice, compassion, and humility. This ethos is making a comeback in business schools through courses on Indian models of management. Ram Rajya is studied not just as a mythological concept, but as a model of ethical governance. Chanakya's Arthashastra is mined for insights on strategic statecraft and economic policy. Stories of Shivaji Maharaj, Buddha, and even modern heroes like E. Sreedharan (the Metro Man of India) are used to teach leadership, innovation, and integrity. These narratives offer students a powerful counterpoint to the dominant Western focus on shareholder capitalism, reminding them that leadership is as much about inner character as outer achievement.

The integration of purpose into business education is also reinforced by the examples of alumni who are redefining what it means to be successful. Increasingly, graduates from IIMs and other elite institutions are choosing to become impact entrepreneurs, ESG consultants, public policy advisors, and education reformers. Their stories of leaving high-paying corporate jobs to pursue meaningful ventures are becoming part of institutional folklore, inspiring younger students to follow suit. These alumni act as purpose ambassadors, mentoring students, funding social initiatives, and contributing to curriculum design. Their presence is a living proof that success and significance can go hand in hand.

Despite these advancements, several challenges persist. The culture of placements continues to dominate, with rankings, salaries, and recruiter preferences shaping student aspirations and institutional priorities. Ethics, while emphasized in the classroom, is not always easy to uphold in competitive and high-pressure environments. The concept of purpose can also be difficult to quantify, making it harder to include in performance metrics and accreditation standards. Many faculty members remain hesitant to adopt non-traditional pedagogies, and few B-schools have a structured framework to integrate Indian ethos into mainstream management education. Yet, the direction is clear. Institutions that prioritize ethics and purpose are attracting not only socially conscious students but also companies seeking values-driven leadership.

The Rise of Purpose-Driven Education

An emerging trend in Indian B-schools is the shift from career ambition to life mission:

Today's students are increasingly:

- ✔ Questioning the role of business in society
- ✔ Seeking meaning in their work
- ✔ Exploring careers in social impact, sustainability, entrepreneurship, and public policy
- ✔ Choosing to work with startups, NGOs, or create ventures with a mission

To support this, B-schools are offering:

 Social immersion programs

 Live consulting projects for non-profits and rural enterprises

 Courses like "Business and Society," "Leadership for Change," "Entrepreneurship for Impact"

 Collaborations with CSR divisions and government initiatives like Atal Innovation Mission and Startup India

This signals a larger shift–*from success to significance.*

One of the strongest indicators of this transformation is the curricular shift seen in leading institutions. Ethics and Corporate Governance are now mandatory. Sustainability and social impact are no longer niche electives but mainstream topics. Programs on mindfulness, self-leadership, and reflective learning are growing in popularity. Courses are being designed around frameworks like the triple bottom line (People, Planet, Profit), and students are encouraged to measure success not just by ROI, but by impact on community and environment. Institutions like TISS, IIM Shillong, and XLRI are leading the way by integrating public systems, development finance, and social justice into their MBA offerings.

This trend is also visible in the growing alignment of Indian business schools with global movements like ESG (Environmental, Social, Governance), SDGs (Sustainable Development Goals), and stakeholder capitalism. From joining the United Nations Global Compact to launching climate labs and ethical business incubators, Indian B-schools are positioning themselves at the forefront of a global conversation on responsible management. In the classrooms of ISB and IIM Bangalore, case studies now involve social enterprises, sustainable innovation, and inclusive growth strategies. Students learn to pitch not just to VCs, but to impact investors and development funds.

As this shift deepens, the role of the MBA is being redefined. It is no longer merely a credential to climb the corporate ladder—it is becoming a toolkit for systemic change. Leadership is taught not as a way to dominate, but as a way to serve. Ethics is no longer abstract but applied. Purpose is not a luxury, but a necessity. The Indian MBA is being recalibrated—not just to build companies, but to build communities and a country. And as India marches toward its vision of becoming a Viksit Bharat by 2047, its business schools will play a critical role in preparing leaders who are not just sharp in strategy but also rooted in service.

Alumni as Purpose Ambassadors

Increasingly, alumni of top Indian B-schools are returning as:

- Impact entrepreneurs
- Climate warriors and ESG champions
- Policy advisors and think tank contributors
- Authors, coaches, and nonprofit leaders

Their stories are shaping a new generation of students who see the MBA as a platform for creating a better world, not just climbing the corporate ladder.

In conclusion, a fundamental transformation underway in Indian management education. Leadership, ethics, and purpose are no longer peripheral concerns—they are becoming central to the very identity of business schools. The Indian MBA is evolving into a platform not just for personal success but for public service. As the next generation of students enters B-school classrooms across the country, they will not just be taught how to lead organizations. They will be inspired to lead lives of meaning, integrity, and purpose. That, perhaps, is the true measure of business education in the new India.

Part V: Looking Ahead

CHAPTER FIFTEEN

Globalizing Indian B-Schools:

Taking Indian Management Education to the World Stage: India, known for producing some of the world's most influential CEOs and global business leaders, has traditionally seen its business schools focused on serving domestic needs. For decades, Indian B-schools were built to cater to national industries, family-run enterprises, and public sector undertakings. However, with India's growing economic might and deeper integration into global markets, the role and aspirations of Indian management institutions have evolved. No longer content with being regional champions, India's leading B-schools are stepping onto the world stage, eager to showcase not only their academic rigor but also their unique value systems, research, and management philosophies. In the 21st century, the globalization of Indian B-schools is no longer a choice—it is a necessity to remain competitive and relevant.

The push toward international recognition began with a desire to benchmark Indian business schools against global standards. With top Indian talent increasingly working across borders, it became imperative for institutions to produce globally competent managers who could thrive in diverse business environments. The race to secure international accreditations became a hallmark of this ambition. Accreditations like AACSB, AMBA, and EQUIS became the gold standard for global credibility. Institutions such as the Indian School of Business (ISB), IIM Calcutta, IIM Indore, and SPJIMR proudly joined the ranks of globally accredited schools. These accreditations signaled to the world that Indian B-schools were capable of delivering education on par with the best institutions globally—ensuring high standards in governance, curriculum, research, faculty, and student outcomes.

The Push Toward International Recognition

Globalization of Indian B-schools has been driven by several factors:

- ⊘ Aspiration to match global benchmarks

- ⊘ Attracting international students and faculty

- ⊘ Enhancing placement opportunities with multinational companies

- ⊘ Improving positions in international rankings

- ⊘ Creating knowledge that influences global management thought

Institutions began to ask:

How can we make Indian B-schools as desirable as INSEAD, LBS, or Harvard—not just for Indians, but for students and executives worldwide?

The next leap came in the form of international rankings. Featuring in the Financial Times (FT), QS, Bloomberg Businessweek, and The Economist global rankings allowed Indian institutions to break free from regional perception. ISB, IIM Ahmedabad, IIM Bangalore, and IIM Calcutta began to secure respectable positions in these prestigious lists. ISB's one-year Post Graduate Programme (PGP) consistently ranked among the top 30 globally, especially in alumni career progression and international mobility. IIM Ahmedabad and IIM Bangalore earned recognition for their rigorous pedagogy and world-class alumni network. These rankings not only amplified the brand of Indian B-schools but also made them attractive to international applicants and collaborators.

Crucial to the globalization journey has been the forging of strategic global partnerships. Indian B-schools have formed alliances with elite institutions such as Wharton, Kellogg, LBS, HEC Paris, ESADE, and NUS. These collaborations enabled faculty exchange, joint research, dual degree offerings, and student mobility. IIM Ahmedabad's ties with ESSEC and Columbia, ISB's founding partnerships with Wharton and Kellogg, and SPJIMR's collaboration with Brandeis and Michigan State have all added significant global exposure to their students. These programs aren't merely symbolic; they are transformational, providing Indian students with insights into international markets, diverse work cultures, and alternative management styles.

Another marker of globalization is the growing presence of international faculty and students on Indian campuses. While the numbers are still modest, institutions like ISB and IIMs have begun attracting students from South Asia, Africa, and the Middle East, especially in executive and short-term programs. Faculty from global universities are invited for visiting lectureships, case competitions, and research residencies. These engagements enrich classroom conversations and introduce multiple global perspectives to Indian students. Similarly, outbound mobility has increased, with Indian students participating in global immersion programs, semester exchanges, and summer internships across continents.

Globalization has also reshaped research priorities. Indian B-schools are no longer content with only publishing in domestic journals. They now actively contribute to top-tier international journals and research forums. The focus areas often align with India's strengths—emerging markets, frugal innovation, inclusive growth, and digital transformation. Faculty from ISB, IIMs, and XLRI are now presenting at conferences like the Academy of Management and publishing in journals like Harvard Business Review, Journal of International Business Studies, and Strategic Management Journal. This has elevated India's voice in the global management discourse.

However, this journey has not been without challenges. Indian B-schools still face perception issues globally. Despite producing top talent, the institutions themselves are often overshadowed by their alumni. Visa constraints, mobility barriers, and a lack of brand recognition outside South Asia limit the ability to attract international students at scale. The dominance of a few elite schools also means that globalization efforts are uneven, with many second-tier institutions struggling to catch up due to limited resources or strategic vision. Additionally, credit transfer issues, lack of global funding models, and dependence on local placements make it difficult to fully internationalize the MBA experience.

Government policy has started to play a supportive role. Initiatives like Study in India, GIAN (Global Initiative of Academic Networks), and NEP 2020 have created frameworks for greater international academic exchange. The NEP's push for multidisciplinary education, academic autonomy, and institutional collaboration provides a fertile ground for innovation. The government's openness to foreign universities setting up campuses in India also signals a shift in mindset—from insular protectionism to collaborative excellence. Indian B-schools, with the right support, can become not only exporters of talent but also importers of ideas, practices, and innovation.

The Role of Government and Policy

India's National Education Policy (NEP) 2020 and initiatives like Study in India and GIAN (Global Initiative of Academic Networks) encourage:

International faculty visits and joint courses

Establishing foreign university campuses in India

Promoting India as a global education hub

Creating an ecosystem for cross-border academic exchange

With these enablers, Indian B-schools are well-positioned to export their models and attract global learners.

An important aspect of globalization is ensuring it doesn't come at the cost of Indian identity. The most impactful Indian B-schools are those that blend global excellence with local wisdom. They use international tools to solve Indian problems, and Indian frameworks to contribute to global thought. The globalization of Indian B-schools is not about mimicking the West, but about showcasing India's unique strengths—its diversity, resilience, entrepreneurial energy, and civilizational depth. This is evident in how institutions like IIM Kozhikode position themselves with the theme "India for the World," or how SPJIMR embeds Indian values into global leadership programs.

Looking ahead, the future of Indian B-schools on the global stage looks promising. The demand for management education in Asia, Africa, and Latin America is rising, and India is well-positioned to lead. Its English-speaking academic ecosystem, cost-effective delivery, and talent pool offer a unique competitive advantage. The road ahead lies in making internationalization broad-based and inclusive—ensuring not just a few but many Indian institutions become globally relevant.

In conclusion, globalizing Indian B-schools is a journey of balancing tradition with transformation. It requires vision, investment, and a mindset shift. But as India aspires to become a Viksit Bharat by 2047, its business schools have a vital role to play. Not just in preparing global managers, but in shaping global management thinking. The Indian MBA of the future will not just teach how to manage companies—it will teach how to lead with conscience, build with inclusion, and think with a global mind and a Bharatiya soul.

New-Age MBAs: Skills for the Future

The 21st century has ushered in a new era where the pace of change is unprecedented. Technology is transforming industries overnight, the workforce is becoming borderless, and the meaning of work itself is evolving. In this dynamic landscape, the traditional MBA program—once seen as a golden passport to corporate success—is being redefined. No longer can Indian B-schools afford to focus solely on legacy models rooted in functional silos and outdated frameworks. The world now demands agile leaders, not just competent managers; entrepreneurs, not just executives; visionaries, not just strategists. Thus, the idea of a "New-Age MBA" has taken root—an MBA designed to equip students not just for the jobs of today but for the leadership challenges of tomorrow.

Historically, MBA programs were tailored to feed structured corporate hierarchies. Students specialized in finance, marketing, operations, or HR and entered predictable career tracks in banking, FMCG, consulting, or manufacturing. But the present landscape is far less linear. The rise of digital platforms, artificial intelligence, gig work, sustainability imperatives, and purpose-led business models is rewriting the playbook. The professional of the future needs a vastly different toolkit—one that blends analytical rigor with emotional intelligence, technological literacy with human-centered design, and entrepreneurial daring with ethical grounding. Indian business schools, to remain relevant and impactful, must pivot boldly to meet this demand.

Why the Traditional MBA is No Longer Enough

Historically, an MBA prepared students for predictable career paths in:

- Banking and finance
- Marketing and sales
- Operations and HR
- Consulting and corporate strategy

But today's world demands more:

- Agility over certainty
- Problem-solving over process execution
- Tech fluency over traditional specialization
- Purpose-driven work over profit-driven roles
- Collaboration across cultures, sectors, and disciplines

This shift is forcing B-schools to reimagine the MBA from being a static credential to a dynamic, skills-based growth journey.

A key characteristic of the New-Age MBA is fluency in technology and data. Business decisions today are driven by dashboards, not just boardrooms. To remain competitive, MBAs must now be conversant in analytics tools like Python, R, Power

BI, and Tableau. Courses in AI, machine learning, blockchain applications, and cybersecurity are increasingly becoming part of core MBA curricula. Institutions like ISB and IIM Bangalore are leading the charge, offering specialized tracks in digital transformation and business analytics. Meanwhile, schools such as Great Lakes Institute of Management have launched full-fledged programs focused on AI and data science. The message is clear: if you're not fluent in tech, you're functionally illiterate in the business world.

Alongside technological acumen, innovation and creativity are now essential. The inclusion of design thinking, customer experience mapping, and problem-framing exercises in MBA pedagogy signals this shift. Indian B-schools are partnering with global innovation hubs and IDEO-style labs to expose students to rapid prototyping and solution-centric methodologies. At institutes like IIM Bangalore and Srishti Manipal, students now work in interdisciplinary teams to tackle real-world problems with empathy and innovation—skills that cannot be taught through textbooks alone but must be experienced hands-on.

The entrepreneurial mindset is another pillar of the New-Age MBA. With India's startup ecosystem booming, business schools are not just training job-seekers but nurturing job creators. Campuses now host incubators, accelerators, and demo days where student ventures pitch to real investors. From IIM Ahmedabad's Centre for Innovation Incubation and Entrepreneurship (CIIE) to ISB's DLabs, the infrastructure to support entrepreneurship has matured significantly. Courses on lean startup methodology, MVP development, and digital scaling are mainstream. Placement deferment options allow budding founders to pursue their ventures with institutional backing and the security of future recruitment if needed. Indian MBAs today are as likely to build the next fintech unicorn as they are to join a consulting firm.

In an era where businesses are under increasing scrutiny to align with societal and environmental goals, the understanding of sustainability and ESG (Environmental, Social, and Governance) principles is non-negotiable. Indian B-schools are responding by embedding ESG frameworks into core courses. Students are learning to assess climate risks, design circular economy models, and report sustainability performance using global standards like GRI and BRSR. Institutions such as XLRI, SPJIMR, and IIM Udaipur have made sustainability a defining feature of their programs, offering electives and live projects that tackle issues like ethical sourcing, green finance, and inclusive innovation. The next generation of business leaders is being taught to view profit not as an end, but as a means to impact.

While data and digital tools are indispensable, it is human-centered skills that will differentiate truly effective leaders. As automation handles routine tasks, uniquely human capabilities like emotional intelligence, ethical judgment, cross-cultural collaboration, and storytelling become critical. MBA programs are therefore introducing reflective labs, leadership development workshops, and mindfulness modules to build these competencies. Students engage in value clarification exercises, work on projects in underserved communities, and navigate complex dilemmas in role-play scenarios. The goal is to nurture professionals who lead not just with logic but with empathy and purpose.

Pedagogical innovation is underpinning this transformation. Traditional lectures are giving way to flipped classrooms, where students consume content online and use class time for application. Simulation games, consulting labs, and field immersions provide experiential learning. Modular and stackable formats allow students to personalize their learning journey, and lifelong learning is encouraged through alumni-accessible micro-credentials. At schools like SPJIMR and Ashoka University, the MBA is no longer confined to two years on campus—it is a continuous, evolving experience that adapts with the learner's career and aspirations.

Career services are also evolving to support this new paradigm. The idea of a linear career trajectory is being replaced by portfolio careers. MBAs today may start in consulting, transition to a startup, pivot into policy, and eventually build a social enterprise. Business schools are supporting this shift by appointing career architects rather than just placement officers. Students are guided to build long-term career capital—through internships, certifications, networking, and impact projects. Roles in climate tech, healthtech, creator economy, and public leadership are being actively explored, alongside traditional corporate options.

The integration of EdTech platforms and industry certifications is also a game-changer. B-schools are collaborating with players like UpGrad, Coursera, and Emeritus to offer globally co-branded courses. Certifications in Six Sigma, CFA, Agile, and Google Analytics are being embedded into MBA programs. These alliances allow students to build job-ready skills while retaining academic rigor. Co-teaching models involving industry practitioners are breaking down the ivory tower mentality of academia, bringing real-world challenges into the classroom.

Another defining feature of the New-Age MBA is the increasing agency of students in shaping their own education. Students are no longer passive recipients of knowledge; they are active co-creators. From initiating clubs and community projects to launching podcasts and publications, they are contributing to the institution's intellectual capital. Student governments influence curriculum changes, mentor juniors, and co-host international conferences. This culture of ownership creates not just learners, but leaders.

In sum, the New-Age MBA represents a radical reimagination of what business education should be. It is not merely about acquiring a degree or landing a job. It is about preparing for a world of volatility, complexity, and opportunity. It is about building leaders who are as comfortable with spreadsheets as they are with sustainability reports, who understand both balance sheets and behavioral science, who can code in Python and speak with purpose. Indian B-schools, by embracing this evolution, are not just responding to market trends—they are shaping the future of leadership itself.

As we look ahead, the success of the New-Age MBA will be measured not by rankings or placement figures, but by the problems its graduates solve, the organizations they build, and the values they uphold. In this lies the true purpose of management education—not to churn out corporate climbers, but to cultivate changemakers. And in doing so, Indian business schools will not only remain relevant in the global landscape, but lead it with conviction, creativity, and conscience.

The Future-Ready Skillset: What New-Age MBAs Must Master

1. Digital & Tech Fluency

Business leaders must now speak the language of data and technology. New-age MBAs are being trained in:

- Data analytics & visualization (Power BI, Tableau, Python)
- AI, machine learning, and automation in business
- Blockchain applications in supply chain and finance
- Cybersecurity and digital ethics
- Digital marketing and influencer economies

2. Design Thinking & Innovation

Courses in design thinking, creative problem-solving, and user experience (UX) are becoming core to many MBA programs. These skills help students:

- Solve complex, undefined problems
- Prototype ideas rapidly
- Build customer-centric solutions

3. Entrepreneurial Mindset

Whether or not a student becomes a startup founder, they must think like one. This includes:

- Opportunity recognition
- Lean startup methodologies
- Pitching and fundraising
- Growth hacking and digital scaling
- Learning through startup incubators and accelerators

Institutions like ISB, IIM Bangalore, and SPJIMR are actively fostering entrepreneurship cells, startup weekends, and seed fund access.

4. Sustainability & ESG Literacy

The leaders of tomorrow must understand how to:

- Build sustainable business models
- Align strategy with Environmental, Social & Governance (ESG) goals
- Measure and report impact using global standards (like GRI or BRSR)
- Tackle climate risks, circular economy models, and responsible consumption

This is not just a trend—it's a business imperative.

5. Human-Centered Skills

In an AI-driven world, what remains uniquely human will be most valuable. MBAs of the future must be trained in:

- Emotional intelligence
- Cross-cultural collaboration
- Conflict resolution and empathy-based leadership
- Ethical decision-making and mindfulness
- Adaptive communication and storytelling

CHAPTER SEVENTEEN

Beyond the Metro: Democratizing Business Education

Taking Management Learning to Bharat's Heartland: For decades, India's business education landscape has been dominated by elite institutions located in metropolitan cities. These urban centers—Mumbai, Delhi, Bengaluru, Kolkata, Chennai, and Hyderabad—boasted not only the most reputed B-schools but also the most extensive networks of recruiters, alumni, and corporate partnerships. Their prestige was matched by their exclusivity. For students from Tier 2 and Tier 3 towns, especially those from economically or linguistically marginalized backgrounds, accessing this world of polished MBA corridors often meant overcoming daunting odds. As a result, management education in India evolved with a significant urban bias. However, in recent years, a quiet but powerful shift has taken root: the democratization of business education. India is witnessing a movement to bring management learning to every corner of Bharat, beyond metro borders and into the heart of small towns, villages, and districts where the majority of India's youth resides.

The Urban Bias in Traditional Business Education: The challenges of access have historically been structural and cultural. The top business schools in metros were better resourced, taught in English, and assumed a level of prior exposure to corporate jargon, digital tools, and global thinking that many students from rural backgrounds simply did not have. Admission into these schools required more than just merit; it demanded social capital, financial capability, and linguistic fluency. As a result, countless talented youth from smaller towns were either denied access or forced to migrate, often at great personal and familial sacrifice. This not only led to brain drain from rural areas but also perpetuated the divide between India and Bharat.

To bridge this gap, the democratization of business education is being driven by a multi-pronged approach. First, there has been a significant increase in the establishment of new institutions in smaller cities and towns. The newer IIMs—located in Udaipur, Trichy, Ranchi, Kashipur, and Bodh Gaya—have made deliberate efforts to attract regional talent and integrate local economic ecosystems into their pedagogy. Alongside these public institutions, private universities such as GIM in Goa, IFMR in Sri City, and KIIT in Bhubaneswar have also played pivotal roles in decentralizing the MBA dream. These institutions are redefining excellence in education not as something confined to geography, but something rooted in purpose and inclusion.

Second, digital learning has emerged as a powerful equalizer. With the explosion of internet penetration and smartphone usage in Tier 2 and 3 cities, EdTech platforms like UpGrad, Coursera, BYJU'S, and SWAYAM are reaching students who might never physically step onto a metro campus. B-schools have responded with hybrid models, online MBA programs, and regional learning centers. The COVID-19 pandemic accelerated this transition, forcing traditional institutions to go online and making high-quality faculty accessible across geographies. For the first time, a management aspirant in Saharanpur or Silchar can take a course in strategic management from a professor in Ahmedabad or Boston without leaving home.

New Institutions in New Geographies

In recent years, several B-schools and universities have emerged in smaller cities, with a clear mission to serve regional talent:

- IIMs in Tiruchirappalli, Udaipur, Kashipur, Bodh Gaya, and Jammu

- Private institutions like GIM (Goa), KIIT (Bhubaneswar), IFMR (Sri City), and DSB (Dehradun)

- State universities and autonomous colleges launching MBA programs with local industry linkages

These institutions are proving that excellence need not be urban, and that leadership can be cultivated anywhere.

Yet, democratization is not only about location or modality—it's about mindset. A major hurdle for many students from non-metro backgrounds is language. Most Indian MBA programs are conducted in English, which creates psychological barriers for students educated in vernacular mediums. Institutions must address this by incorporating bilingual support, vernacular resources, and contextualized pedagogy that respects and reflects local realities. Business education needs to be linguistically inclusive, culturally sensitive, and confidence-building for students who may be first-generation graduates or learners from disadvantaged backgrounds.

One of the most exciting developments in this movement is the surge of entrepreneurial training in rural and semi-urban India. Empowering students to become job creators rather than just job seekers is a game-changer. Initiatives such as Startup India, Atal Innovation Mission, and the proliferation of incubation centers across state universities have brought the language of entrepreneurship to the grassroots. Institutions like IRMA (Anand), XISS (Ranchi), TISS (Tuljapur), and Deshpande Foundation (Hubballi) are actively nurturing local entrepreneurs with contextual business models in agri-tech, rural fintech, ed-tech, and social innovation. These programs focus not just on profit, but on solving pressing social problems with scalable, sustainable solutions.

Democratizing business education also involves aligning curriculum with local industry. Management programs in Coimbatore may focus on textiles and family-run businesses, while those in Ludhiana might explore logistics and manufacturing. Regional industry-academia collaboration can ensure that students receive education that is locally relevant, skill-oriented, and directly employable. Such partnerships also help in facilitating internships and live projects that offer real-world exposure to students without forcing them to migrate to distant metros.

Government policies have been instrumental in this transformation. The National Education Policy (NEP) 2020 emphasizes access, equity, and multilingual education. It also promotes credit transfers and modular degree programs, allowing students to build their careers in a flexible, step-by-step manner. Rashtriya Uchchatar Shiksha Abhiyan (RUSA) is strengthening infrastructure in state universities, while AICTE and UGC reforms are pushing institutions to develop regional outreach and incubation capabilities. Initiatives like the Academic Bank of Credits (ABC), digital universities, and skill-integrated degrees are reshaping the landscape to favor learners in remote and under-resourced regions.

Social enterprises and non-profit organizations have also stepped into the void, especially where formal institutions are lagging. Deshpande Foundation's LEAD program, iDreamCareer's career guidance for rural youth, and Gandhi Fellowship's leadership training have brought management thinking to corners of the country often ignored by mainstream academia. They work closely with communities, offer mentoring in vernacular languages, and foster grassroots innovation. Their interventions bridge the gap between aspiration and access, proving that talent exists everywhere if only opportunity is made available.

The ripple effects of this movement are already visible. B-school graduates from Tier 2 and 3 cities are now launching startups, joining global companies, and influencing local governance and policy. Institutions in these cities are producing their own success stories—alumni who return as faculty, mentors, or investors, thereby fueling a virtuous cycle of empowerment. The ecosystem is growing not just in scale but in diversity, richness, and relevance. Importantly, this decentralization of management education is shifting the perception of leadership from an urban preserve to a national responsibility.

However, challenges remain. Many smaller institutions struggle with faculty recruitment, research output, infrastructure, and brand visibility. Students still face societal pressures and skepticism about career prospects from local MBAs. Employers often perceive a hierarchy between metros and non-metros when recruiting talent. To address this, a cultural shift is needed in how we define prestige, merit, and success in education. We must celebrate and amplify stories of rural achievers, local entrepreneurs, and community innovators as much as we do corporate executives from global cities.

Language, Confidence and Inclusion

Democratization also means tust sýrmbṛiares in business education for non-metro youth, it also brough challenges:

- Teaching business principies in regional languages

- Offering soft skills and communication training tailored to rural learners

- Encouraging first-generation learners to see themselves as capable leaders

- Promoting role models from Tier 2 and 3 towns who have made it big

Programs like AICTE's regional MBA courses, IGNOU's open business degrees, and local entrepreneurial summits are helping build confidence in context

In the years to come, the role of Indian business schools must evolve from merely producing managers to nurturing socially conscious, locally embedded, and globally competent leaders. These leaders should not just be comfortable in boardrooms but also capable of transforming mandis, gram panchayats, and small-town enterprises. Management education must redefine its mission: not just preparing students for corporate careers, but equipping them to build a better Bharat.

The democratization of business education is not a peripheral experiment—it is central to India's aspirations for inclusive development and equitable growth. It ensures that leadership talent emerges not just from polished campuses but from every PIN code, every caste, every community, and every corner of the country. As we march toward Viksit Bharat 2047, it is these grassroots managers, ethical entrepreneurs, and first-generation MBAs who will carry the torch forward. Their education must be world-class not despite their geography, but because of it. This is the future of Indian management education—local in access, national in spirit, and global in ambition.

CHAPTER EIGHTEEN

India's Business Education by 2047: A Vision

As India moves steadily toward the historic milestone of 2047, marking a century since gaining independence, its education systems face a unique responsibility: to not only reflect the aspirations of a New India but also help shape its trajectory. Among the pillars of national progress, business education stands out as a vital force capable of shaping leaders, builders, entrepreneurs, and policy thinkers who will define the future. The world in 2047 will be more technologically advanced, environmentally conscious, globally interconnected, and socially complex than anything Indian B-schools have seen before. This demands a new vision—bold, inclusive, and transformational.

Indian business schools can no longer afford to be degree factories focused solely on placements. They must transform into leadership ecosystems that empower students to become lifelong learners, responsible decision-makers, ethical entrepreneurs, and inclusive nation-builders. The mission is clear: redefine the MBA as a platform not just for profit but for purpose, not merely for job-seeking but for change-making.

From Degree Factories to Leadership Ecosystems The very architecture of business education must evolve. The future B-school will not be confined to a classroom or a campus but will function as a dynamic ecosystem where learning is personalized, continuous, and impact-driven.

A Call Beyond the MBA

By 2047, the question may no longer be "Which B-school did you go to?" but rather, "What kind of problems have you solved?

Business education must evolve from:

From	To
Degrees	Lifelong learning journeys
Placements	Purposeful career creation
Corporate-centric focus	Nation- and planet-centric leadership
Urban elitism	Mass democratization and inclusion
Siloed disciplines	Interdisciplinary, integrative thinking
Western mimicry	Indian innovation and thought leadership
Indian innovation	Indian innovation and thought leadership

Modular, interdisciplinary programs will replace rigid two-year formats. Students will be encouraged to enter and exit the education system at multiple points in their careers, armed with micro-degrees, project experience, and new-age credentials.

Leadership development will extend far beyond PowerPoint presentations and group discussions. It will emphasize self-awareness, collaboration, ethical judgment, and resilience in the face of crisis. MBA programs will need to integrate leadership labs, social immersions, and mentorship modules that push students to work in rural communities, startups, and policy think tanks—preparing them to lead not just in the boardroom, but in society.

Indian Thought, Global Relevance: As India reclaims its civilizational identity and emerges as a voice of balance in a fractured global order, its B-schools must develop original Indian management frameworks. Concepts like Dharma (righteous conduct), Karma Yoga (selfless action), and Vasudhaiva Kutumbakam (the world is one family) have profound implications for leadership, sustainability, and corporate ethics.

Instead of mimicking Western models, Indian B-schools should begin exporting indigenous thought through global case studies, journals, and collaborative programs. India has valuable lessons in frugal innovation, spiritual leadership, cooperative economics, and inclusive capitalism. These ideas are not only Bharatiya in origin but universally relevant in a world seeking sustainable and humane alternatives to unbridled capitalism.

Technology as a Teaching Partner AI will not replace teachers, but it will revolutionize how they teach. Adaptive learning platforms powered by artificial intelligence will personalize content delivery, assessments, and feedback. Augmented Reality (AR) and Virtual Reality (VR) will create immersive case simulations and experiential learning opportunities, making classrooms interactive and global.

Blockchain will verify credentials, maintain learning records, and support transparent assessment systems. AI tutors will assist faculty in identifying learning gaps, while voice-to-text and translation tools will democratize learning across languages. Yet, in this tech-infused future, the human element must remain sacred. Faculty will shift from being content deliverers to becoming coaches, mentors, and moral guides.

Hyperlocal and Hyperglobal The future of Indian management education must be simultaneously hyperlocal and hyperglobal. While B-schools must establish campuses in every district to train grassroots entrepreneurs, agricultural innovators, and cooperative leaders, they must also forge global partnerships with universities across the U.S., Europe, Africa, and Asia to enable research exchange, dual degrees, and cultural cross-pollination.

This model prepares students to solve local problems with a global mindset. A business school in Nagaland must teach entrepreneurship for tribal artisans while enabling international exchange with fashion schools in Italy. A campus in Odisha must train climate entrepreneurs while collaborating with Dutch universities on water management.

Sustainability and Ethics at the Core Every future MBA curriculum must be rooted in ethics, ESG (Environmental, Social, and Governance), and social impact. These should not be electives but the foundation upon which marketing, strategy, and finance are taught. B-schools must evolve into sustainability think tanks that work with governments, nonprofits, and businesses to tackle climate change, poverty, and inequality.

THE VISION: WHAT SHOULD INDIAN B-SCHOOLS LOOK LIKE BY 2047?

GLOBALLY TOP-RANKED, BHARATIYA AT HEART

Blend global academic excellence with Indian civilizational wisdom

MANAGEMENT FOR NATION-BUILDING, NOT JUST PROFIT

Solve India's developmental challenges through business leadership

POWERED BY TECHNOLOGY, ROOTED IN VALUES

Embrace AI and hybrid learning, while nurturing ethics and empathy

INDIA AS A GLOBAL EDUCATION HUB

Attract and foster students from across the world

B-SCHOOLS IN EVERY REGION, FOR EVERY INDIAN

Expand access to world-class business education nationwide

Tomorrow's managers must be equipped to measure not just EBITDA, but carbon footprints and impact scores. Business strategy must consider regenerative economies, circular value chains, and ethical governance. The Indian MBA must symbolize stewardship over short-termism.

The Faculty of the Future The teacher of tomorrow will wear many hats—researcher, mentor, industry collaborator, public thinker, and digital content creator. Faculty will co-design courses with industry experts and global practitioners. Case writing and applied research will receive as much importance as journal publications. Universities will invest in faculty development through exposure to startups, government projects, and international academic residencies.

AI may handle grading and analytics, but the mentorship and intellectual stimulation offered by great teachers will remain irreplaceable. In fact, as learning becomes more virtual, the faculty's role in shaping values, inspiring inquiry, and guiding transformation will only grow.

Entrepreneurship for All India's demographic dividend and startup ecosystem demand that every MBA student graduates with an entrepreneurial mindset. This doesn't mean every student has to launch a company, but they must learn to think independently, embrace risk, solve real problems, and create value.

B-schools must house incubators, offer seed grants, and support venture creation as seriously as they support placements. A national grid of B-school incubators could create tens of thousands of local enterprises across India's districts, accelerating job creation and inclusive development.

Inclusion Through Language and Access To truly democratize business education, India must make the MBA accessible to all—regardless of geography, gender, caste, or economic background. Offering MBA programs in regional languages is a powerful step forward. With AI-driven translation and speech-to-text tools, high-quality business content can now be delivered in

Hindi, Tamil, Bengali, Marathi, and beyond.

Institutions must ensure that digital access is not just available but empowering. Scholarships, mentorship networks, and preparatory programs will be key to integrating first-generation learners from rural and tribal areas. The MBA of 2047 must be a gateway for Bharat's youth to lead India's growth story.

Business Education as Nation Building Business education must be repositioned as a form of national service. Students should spend part of their curriculum working with Panchayats, cooperatives, social enterprises, or government departments. Leadership must be cultivated in the field, not just in the classroom. Solving real problems in sanitation, rural livelihoods, urban infrastructure, or education policy must become integral to the MBA journey.

This service orientation can create a generation of purpose-driven leaders who view their degree not as a ticket to privilege but as a responsibility toward their community and country.

Strategic Enablers for the Vision To realize this bold future, we need systemic support. A National Business Education Mission (NBEM) should be launched to integrate policy, funding, and innovation. Public-Private Partnerships (PPPs) must fund incubation labs, rural MBA hubs, and digital learning platforms.

AICTE and UGC must be reimagined as enabling bodies that encourage innovation and accountability. Rankings must evolve to measure impact: graduates placed in social enterprises, startups created, rural internships completed, or carbon credits saved. This shift from input metrics to outcome impact will redefine success.

India as a Global Hub of Management Thought By 2047, India can and should become the world's preferred destination for values-driven, future-ready business education. Students from across Asia, Africa, and Latin America must look to India not just for cost-effective MBAs but for culturally conscious, ethically grounded, and globally relevant education. Indian B-schools can offer an alternative vision of business leadership rooted in compassion, community, and sustainability.

A Future Rooted in Purpose and Possibility The question is no longer whether Indian business education will grow—it is whether it will lead. The future of the MBA must not be about bigger salaries, shinier campuses, or more global tie-ups. It must be about building leaders who are as committed to the nation as they are to the market.

By the time India turns 100, the Indian MBA should represent more than a degree. It should be a badge of wisdom, responsibility, and purpose. If done right, Indian business schools won't just prepare graduates to serve the world's top corporations. They will prepare them to serve the world itself.

This is the mission. This is the promise. This is the future of Indian business education.

Epilogue: The Saga Continues - Business Education In The Amrit Kaal

As India steps into its Amrit Kaal—the 25-year period from 2022 to 2047, leading up to its centenary of independence—it stands at the threshold of extraordinary possibilities. With a demographic dividend, a digital revolution, and a renewed sense of national purpose, Bharat is poised to take its place as a Viksit Rashtra—a developed, self-confident, and globally respected nation.

In this grand journey, business education is not a bystander—it is a catalyst.

The story of business schools in India, from humble beginnings to global ambitions, mirrors India's own evolution—from survival to strategy, from imitation to innovation, from dependency to self-reliance.

But the work is far from over.

What Lies Ahead

The coming decades will test the very foundations of management education:

- Can we produce leaders who heal, not just lead?
- Can we embed Indian values in global strategy?
- Can we train students not just to earn, but to serve, solve, and sustain?
- Can we turn every B-school into a nation-building lab—where ideas are born, institutions are shaped, and futures are forged?

The answer must be yes. Because the world no longer needs just more MBAs—it needs meaningful, mission-driven, and morally anchored leaders.

From B-School to Bharat-School: The future of Indian business education is not merely about scaling up; it's about transforming the purpose of education itself. It's time we see our B-schools not just as career gateways, but as Bharat-schools—places that produce leaders who are:

- Rooted in Dharma, driven by purpose
- Fluent in data, but guided by wisdom
- Equally at ease in corporate boardrooms and rural enterprises
- Champions of Atmanirbhar Bharat, builders of Vasudhaiva Kutumbakam

A Final Word

This saga is not just about institutions—it is about people:
The faculty who chose classrooms over corporations.
The students who dared to dream beyond their backgrounds.
The entrepreneurs who defied odds and built legacies.
The reformers who shaped policy and steered vision.
And the next generation—you, the reader—who will carry the torch forward.

May the business schools of India never forget that their highest purpose is not placement, but upliftment. Not just success, but significance. Not just careers, but contributions to the nation and the world.

The saga continues. And Bharat leads the way.

About The Author

Ashish Gupta is a visionary educator, author, and thought leader in the field of higher education and business school transformation in India. With over 14 years of leadership experience in the Indian university ecosystem with brands like O.P. Jindal Global University, RV University, etc, in the domains like Admissions, Outreach & International Relations, and strategic initiatives in alumni engagement and global partnerships.

A firm believer in the power of education to drive national development, Ashish has dedicated his career to democratizing access to quality business education, especially for students from Tier 2 and Tier 3 cities. He is the founder of BharatMBA with the vision of building a skills-based entry system to B schools over entrance exams.

As an author, Ashish has written extensively on themes such as career guidance, personal development, Indian leadership models, and the Indianization of management education. His mission is to create a new generation of ethical, entrepreneurial, and India-rooted professionals who can lead in a globalized world with clarity, compassion, and purpose.

He is also the force behind initiatives like The B-School Yatra, a nationwide journey to map the opportunities and challenges facing Indian management education, and Mission Viksit Bharat, which aims to align youth development with India's 2047 development goals.

Through his books, training programs, and policy dialogues, Ashish continues to redefine what it means to be an educator in 21st-century Bharat—blending modern tools with timeless values to inspire a generation that will shape the future of India and the world.

www.ingramcontent.com/pod-product-compliance
Lightning Source LLC
Chambersburg PA
CBHW031135130726
47988CB00006B/2381